LEGENDOTES OF HYDERABAD

LEGENDOTES OF HYDERABAD

NARENDRA LUTHER

NIYOGI BOOKS

Published by
NIYOGI BOOKS
Block D, Building No. 77,
Okhla Industrial Area, Phase-I,
New Delhi-110 020, INDIA
Tel: 91-11-26816301, 26818960
Email: niyogibooks@gmail.com
Website: www.niyogibooksindia.com

Editor: Gita Rajan
Design: Shashi Bhushan Prasad

ISBN: 978-93-83098-17-0
Publication: 2014
First reprint: 2019
Second reprint: 2024

Printed at: Niyogi Offset Pvt. Ltd., New Delhi, India

To my gen next - Rahul, Sandhya and Rajeshwari
And their gen next, Raisa and Rishabh
May my tribe increase!

In vain, O Kings, doth time aspire
To make your names oblivion's sport,
While yonder hill wears like a tiara
The ruined grandeur of your fort.
Though centuries falter and decline,
Your proven strongholds shall remain
Embodied memories of your line,
Incarnate legends of your reign.

– Sarojini Naidu on Golkonda Fort
(1879–1949)

CONTENTS

Pages 2-3: The Chowmahalla Palace
Pages 6-7: Golkonda Fort
Page 8: The Interior of Falaknuma Palace

INTRODUCTION

Do not rush to Google to seek the meaning of the title of the book. There is no such word. I have coined this compound noun by amalgamating two terms – Legends and Anecdotes.

Let me explain.

A legend is a story from old times about people or events, which may be true or not. An anecdote is a short, interesting, or amusing story about a real person or event. This book is about both these, which I have come across during my life, which was largely lived in Hyderabad – and researches. However, I have checked their truth or historicity as far as possible. The matter within therefore is verifiable. Apart from published sources, I have also done considerable work in the oral history of Hyderabad. That related to matters for which there is no published source. For example the story of Kasim Razvi is drawn on the testimony of his most devoted and steadfast 'disciple', the late Zahid Ali Kamil. He was himself a prosperous lawyer and had very good health at eighty-one when I met him. I was lucky with him because according to him, I seemed to have helped him in some matter when I was the head of the Hyderabad Municipal Corporation. He was initially reluctant and said that he wanted to write Razvi's story himself.

I said that Razvi was a person on whom different views could be taken and so different books written. I also told him that he had not done that so far, and hinted very politely that he did not have much time left to do that. Once he was convinced, he came forth with the minutest details of Razvi's life before the latter's conviction, after his release from jail seven years later and finally leaving Hyderabad after thrusting the presidentship of the *Majlis-e-Ittehad-ul-Musalmeen* on a reluctant late-comer.

Similar was the case with 'A Prophet for India'. When I heard about the extraordinary story of Akbar Yar Jung's speech, it seemed too good to be true. For its verification, I turned to his son, the late Prof Rasheedudin Khan, former professor of Osmania and Jawaharlal Nehru universities, and later a member of Rajya Sabha. He was then at Delhi. He not only confirmed it, but also sent me a copy of his father's original speech in Urdu, a copy of its translation in English, a copy of the clipping of news item of *The Hindu* daily in which it was reported – and an exegesis of the Quran in support of Akbar Yar Jung's logic. With such a proof, there was nothing to

hold me back. When my usual lead to sources, the respected journalist, late Mehboob Husain 'Jigar', saw it in my book a year later, he specially rang me up to say, 'This even I did not know.'

Another interesting example is the Legend of Seven Kulchas connected with the legend of seven generations of Nizams ruling in Hyderabad. The first Nizam whom it relates to, himself contradicted it on record. Despite that, even his progenitors believed it. We have a record of the sixth Nizam approving the design of his flag based on that legend.

In short, I submit that the legendotes in this collection are factually correct.

On the highway of formal history, legends and anecdotes do not get their due credit. However, much of the crucial facts and causes of historical developments lie scattered about in the lanes and by-lanes of history. They are therefore a material factor in any historiography. I hope that the readers of this volume will feel that they have read an episodic history of Hyderabad and have savoured the mood swings of the city and participated in its moments of triumphs and tragedies.

Having said that, let us turn to the subject in hand. I will begin with the historical background.

Alauddin Khilji defeated the Kakatiya dynasty of Warangal in 1323 CE. The Tughlaqs followed the Khiljis on the throne of Delhi. Mohammad Tughlaq's local centurions, rebelled against him for his tyrannous and cruel rule, and established the Bahmani kingdom in 1347. The Bahmani kingdom started breaking up in late 15th Century and five sultanates rose out of its smouldering ashes. The last to do so was the governor of Tilang (Golkonda) province, Sultan Quli in 1518. He founded the Qutb Shahi dynasty with its capital at the fort city of Golkonda. There were eight sultans in the dynasty. Mohammad Quli Qutb Shah became the fifth and the most illustrious ruler of that dynasty at the age of fifteen in 1580. He founded a new city outside the fort in 1591 and named it Bhagnagar, after his beloved Bhagmati. Our stories begin from the founding of the city.

In 1687, the Mughal emperor Aurangzeb defeated the last Qutb Shahi ruler, Tana Shah, and merged the Golkonda sultanate in the Deccan province of the Mughal Empire under a governor located at Aurangabad.

Mir Qamaruddin Khan was the Nizam-ul-Mulk (prime minister of the Mughal Empire). When he defeated Mubariz Khan, and became the governor of the Deccan in 1724, the Mughal Emperor, Mohammad Shah meekly acknowledge his position and conferred the title of 'Asaf Jah' on him. Mohammad Shah acknowledged his position. He virtually became independent without declaring his new status. The 'Asaf Jahi' dynasty is thus dated from 1724 CE. He is counted as the first Nizam and his successors bore the same designation. They are ten in number but only seven are recognised, because the title of Asaf Jah was not conferred upon the three immediate successors of the first Asaf Jah covering the period 1748 to 1762. Out of the rest, the first, the sixth, and the seventh Nizams are best known.

The rule of the Asaf Jahi dynasty ended when India took Police Action against Hyderabad in 1948. The state of Hyderabad then became a part of India.

After the first General Elections in India in 1952, Hyderabad had got its first popular government. In 1956, Hyderabad state became a part of the new and enlarged state of Andhra Pradesh, and the city of Hyderabad became its capital.

Feudalism generates more legends than democracy because the lives of leaders in a democracy are more open to public scrutiny. They thus lack the air of mystery associated with the inhabitants of Camelots.

I have arranged all the legendotes chronologically and given relevant citations for them. A few entries are based on the verbal testimony of what I believe are very reliable sources.

For ease of timeline reference, I have appended the relevant dynastic tables in the case of the first two sections and, after the start of the democratic order, names of chief ministers in the third section.

I thank many friends and sources quoted in this book. My special thanks are due to Dr Nagender Reddy, Director of the Salar Jung Museum, Hyderabad, for his unstinting help in providing information and rare images to embellish my text. My young friend Abhishek Patel, by hobby a culinarian (skilled in the preparation of food and interested in its ancestry), and a keen lensman, not only opened his treasure of rare

Mir Qamaruddin Khan First Nizam of Hyderabad

images for my use, but also went out to locate and click elusive targets in sizzling heat. I am very grateful to him.

I thank my old friends Neelamegham, Kesavan and Sarvar for their crucial help which I always take for granted.

Last, but not least, I would like to thank Nitasha Devasar. She handled two of my earlier books very competently, and was responsible for bringing me to Niyogi Books this time. I have enjoyed the interest and care with which this book was handled in its raw form by the publishing team.

Now, welcome to the fairyland of Legendotes.

Narendra Luther
Hyderabad, 25 February 2013

OLDER THAN THE HIMALAYAS

The interior decoration of the city used to be the rocks spread all over. Some of them can be seen even now. These rocks are 2,500 million years old. The readers are a mere seven to eight million years old.

They are part of the India Peninsular Gneissic (pronounced 'nysic') Complex spread over an area of approximately 20,000 square kilometres covering parts of Andhra Pradesh, Karnataka, and Madhya Pradesh. These rocks sprang from the Earth's crust, which is forty kilometres deep. They are amongst the oldest natural heritages of the world. They are older and more stable than the Himalayas.

They make a fascinating landscape. They have human, animal, and other shapes in different sizes. Some rocks are poised delicately in such gravity-defying positions that one fears they might fall any time. However, they will not. They have weathered physical and chemical action over the millennia. Some rocks look as if giant children were playing with them at house-building. Then, suddenly their mothers summoned them home for their meals. And, they might come back!

The Imperial Gazetteer of 1909 observed that 'around Hyderabad and stretching as far west as Lingampalli, fifteen miles from the city, tors and boulders of fantastic shapes are seen everywhere, composed of basalt and granite piled up in picturesque confusion.'

Tagore's fascination for them is mentioned separately. Gunter Grass, the Noble Laureate for literature, visited Hyderabad in 1986. The prehistoric rocks in Hyderabad captivated him so much that he preferred to see them rather than the man-made monuments like the Golkonda Fort and the Charminar. He sketched many of the wonderful rock formations around the city.

They are part of the ecology of the Deccan. They help form the natural drainage system of the area and are responsible for the existence of many lakes.

After the formation of Andhra Pradesh in 1956, colonisation of Banjara Hills picked up and quarrying of rocks because rampant. Rocks were blasted recklessly. Now there is hardly any unbuilt land left in Banjara

Hills. Later, in Jubilee Hill many fascinating rocks were destroyed in the process of construction of fancy houses.

Some persons concerned at the wanton destruction of rocks founded the 'Society to Save Rocks' in 1996. It started a campaign to save this oldest physical heritage.

Amongst its initiatives was to hold an artists' camp to paint and make sculptures on the theme of rocks in 1998. In 2002, it commissioned an inter-disciplinary team of scientists from the Osmania and the Acharya N. G. Ranga Agricultural University for a survey of three districts around Hyderabad.

The team found rich bio-diversity in rock sites. It noted the presence of 215 species of avis, twenty-four of mammals, twenty-seven of the amphibian and reptilian, and eleven of carnivore. The last group includes jackal, Indian fox, sloth bear, and common mongoose.

The team also recorded ninety species of birds breeding in the rock sites and surrounding areas. Out of them fifty-two species were residual or local migrants, twenty-six were local migrants and forty-seven winter migrants. Beautiful birds can be seen perched in the rocky outcrops in the midst of lakes right in the city in the Hussain Sagar Lake between the twin cities, and in Durgam Cheruvu in Jubilee Hills and Shamirpet Lake, about twenty kilometres on the road to Karimnagar.

Facing Page: Rocks of Hyderabad older than the Himalayas

Another formation *(Courtesy: K. Prabhakar)*

The floristic comparison associated with rocks includes important economic species and rare aromatic and herbal medicinal plants.

A handful of people, following the example of Nawab Mehdi Nawaz Jung, have designed their houses with due deference to these pre-historic rocks. These rocks are even more precious than fauna, flora, and physical structures. Whereas we can clone fauna and flora and renovate buildings, these massive and hard looking rocks, once destroyed, will never grow back again.

Because of the efforts of the Society, the government has declared twenty-four rock formations as protected heritage precincts. However, matching action has not followed.

We therefore face an acute danger of losing this great heritage[1].

THE QUTB SHAHI DYNASTY

(1518-1687)

	Name	Born	Period of Rule
1.	Sultan Quli Qutb-ul-Mulk	–	1518-43
2.	Jamsheed Quli Qutb Shah	–	1543 -50
3.	Subhan Quli Qutb Shah	1543	1550-50
4.	Ibrahim Quli Qutb Shah	1530	1550-80
5.	Muhammad Quli Qutb Shah	1565	1580-1612
6.	Muhammad Qutb Shah	1593	1612-26
7.	Abdullah Qutb Shah	1614	1626-72
8.	Abul Hasan Tana Shah*	-	1672-87

* Deposed in 1687 by Aurangzeb.

BIRTH OF BHAGNAGAR

Hyderabad is to cities what Taj Mahal is to buildings - a monument to love. Both commemorate beloveds - Taj for Mumtaz, Bhagnagar for Bhagmati. There is a major contrast, though. While the celebrated mausoleum symbolises a pining for a departed beloved, the city was a celebration of a union with a beloved.

Late in the 16th Century, the fort city of Golkonda became very congested. Therefore, a new site outside the fort and near the River Musi was located for building a new city. Its founder, Mohammad Quli was born in 1565. He was the son of Sultan Ibrahim Qutb Shah (1550-1580), the fourth ruler of the Qutb Shahi dynasty.

As a teenager, he fell in love with a young, beautiful and accomplished

First meeting of Mohammad Quli Qutb Shah and Bhagmati
Facing page: Charminar, Hyderabad

singer and dancer called Bhagmati. They met when he was riding past a temple and Bhagmati was coming out of it after performing her pooja. Then they started meeting every possible day – Mohammad Quli riding across the river.

One day when the river was in spate and a storm was raging, the prince did not hesitate and put his horse in the river to cross it. When the news reached the sultan, he tried to dissuade Mohammad Quli from continuing his foolhardy venture. Mohammad Quli, however, did not budge. Seeing his son's tenacity, and to ensure his safety, the sultan built a bridge across the river in 1578. That was the first bridge. It still exists and is called 'Purana Pul' (the old bridge).

The bridge withstood the great flood of 1908. Towards the end of 20th Century, it was considered unsafe for heavy traffic. Therefore, a new bridge adjacent to it was built to take the load.

On the death of his father, Mohammad Quli became the sultan in 1580. He is acknowledged as the first Urdu poet with an anthology to his credit. Ten years later, he took up the construction of the new city on the southern bank of the river Musi about eight kilometres from the Golkonda fort.

When it was ready, Mohammad Quli named the city Bhagnagar after his beloved, Bhagmati. He composed a couplet to seek divine blessings for the new city:

Mera shehar logaan soon mamoor kar
Rakhya joon tu darya mein min Ya Sami
(O' God, fill my city with people
As you have the river with fish)

The city had fourteen palaces and 14,000 houses, mosques, inns, and even a hospital. The palaces had quaint names like Sajan Mahal, Nadi Mahal,

Bhagmati, after whom the city was named Bhagnagar

Dad Mahal, and Qutb Mandir. In the last named palace, apart from the sultan, only women were allowed entry. Foreign travellers and chroniclers like Tavernier, Thevenot, Moreland, and others universally praised it for its beauty and green cover. Some even said that it was bigger and better than the great cities of the Mughals, like Agra and Lahore.

The Italian, Abbe Carre observed in 1672:

> 'This is large town ... Bhagnagr (is) full of strangers and merchants. Foreigners and others carry on the trade without restrictions to their nationality or particular business. There is such a concourse of every kind of people, merchandise and riches that the place seems to be the centre of all trade in the East'[2].

The name of Bhagnagar seems to have been changed to Hyderabad after the Mughal conquest in 1687.

Ferishta while calling the city Bhagnagar in 1620 stated that the name was changed within a few years of its founding to Hyderabad[3]. Thevenot also added in 1666 that 'the city is called Bhagnar, the Persians call *Aider-Abad*[4].'

The name Hyderabad was in common use in the beginning of the 18th Century. However, Henry George Briggs[5] in 1861 and Sayyed Hussain Bilgrami and C. Wilson[6] in 1884 wrote that the original name of Hyderabad was Bhagnagar and it was still known by that name by many people, especially the Hindus.

A REPLICA OF HEAVEN

Ferishta, a contemporary historian, tells us that on an auspicious day, Sultan Mohammad Quli Qutb Shah issued a decree that the new city should be 'a replica of heaven and unparalleled in the world'.

Jan Pieper, a German Architect, has quoted chapter and verse of the Quran to show that the plan of the new city was indeed an architectural metaphor for the mythical Islamic heaven.

In Arabic, the word for paradise is '*jannat*'. '*Jannat*' also means garden. It is not surprising therefore, that as against less than three sq. kms of habitation, there was a green cover of about twenty-three sq. kms. The city was laid out on the grid system in the form of a giant double-cross. The cross of the axial streets at Charminar is not in exact correspondence with the cardinal directions. The deviation of the east-west axis from the true east is about ten degrees to the south.

This gives it a direction towards Mecca based on the mosque on the upper floor of Charminar. The second cross is about seventy-six metres away at the Char Kaman. It has four massive arches in four directions. In its centre was a fountain. Originally, this was the focal point of the royal quarters. In the west was the royal area shut off from the main centre by an arch (now

Hyderabad (Bhagnagar): An Artist's impression of the original layout.
Conceived by S.P. Shorey, based on historical accounts. researched by Luther.
Drawings/colour artwork by Akshara Advertising, Hyderabad after Shorey's axonometric drawing.
Copyright©

called *Mitti ka Sher*). By its side was a gate on which hung a curtain of cloth-of-gold. On the opposite side behind the arch (now called *Kali Kaman*), musicians sat on this arch and played *shehnai* five times a day. Beyond that were the barracks of the royal guards. It is this area and the 'meaningful relationship' of a number of architectural elements in it, which, according to Pieper, is based on the Quranic vision of the Garden of Heaven.

In the middle of the Islamic paradise, there is a fountain. From this fountain flow four channels - of pure water, pure milk, pure wine and pure honey. The fountain called *Char-su-ka-Houz* (the fountain with four directions still exists) seems to be symbolic of this fountain and the radiation of four streets an architectural transformation of this image. Old pictures of the area show a garden around the fountain. This was progressively phased out to allow better flow of changing traffic.

Further, in heaven there are two types of trees - *Talh* and *Sidr*. They do not exist on earth. So, coconut and betel nut palm trees were planted to represent the heavenly trees.

Artist's impression of original Layout of Hyderabad based on author's researches

Again, in the Quran there is a mention that the abode of the blessed is enclosed by a very high wall on both sides. According to Pieper, the four arches represented the 'wall'. The two arches – northern and southern – were the watch-posts of the royal guards. They represented the fierce Quranic 'Men of the Wall', and allegories of Paradisian exclusiveness, while the eastern and western arches stood for the Quranic pleasures. The enormous gold curtain on the western arch flowing in the air and the shehnai players on the eastern arch filling the air with the 'nasal' sound of the instrument are taken as symbolic of houris of paradise 'with large black eyes, kept for you, attend the blessed in flowing tents.' They will sing in their nasal voices and play music enchanting the Garden of Eternity with their ethereal melodies.

Finally, the mystery of the double cross is resolved. There is not one paradise but a hierarchy of them. 'There are two gardens yielding flowers and all sorts of luxury for the festive and representative life, while two others are filled with herbs and fruits and other humble amenities of what Pieper calls 'pleasureful civic household.' These two gardens are reserved for those 'who live in peace with their Lord.' Behind the western arch lived the king – the 'lord' and in other quarters lived his subjects – 'in peace with their lord.'

Pieper's thesis seems far-fetched but at the same time is quite convincing. It also corroborates the claim often made by common people that the city was like heaven[7].

It is not for nothing that despite its progressive deterioration over generations, the city still attracts people from all over. Only old-timers talk about their lost paradise.

THE MECCA MASJID

Mohammad Qutb Shah succeeded his uncle and father-in-law Mohammad Quli in 1612. A son was born to him in 1614. He named him Abdullah.

The astrologers cast his horoscope and opined that Abdullah was born under an inauspicious star. They cautioned the sultan that the father and son should not see each other for twelve years. Otherwise, grave consequences would follow.

To lift or at least mitigate the curse imposing such a cruel and long prohibition, Mohammad took up the building of a grand mosque in 1617.

He announced that anyone who had not missed any of the five daily prayers prescribed by Islam would lay the foundation stone of the mosque. When no one came forward, he got up and declared that since the age of twelve, he had not missed any prayer. Accordingly, he himself laid the foundation stone.

He had some bricks made out of the earth brought from Mecca and placed over the central arch. The mosque therefore got the name of Mecca Masjid.

The construction of the mosque was very slow and went on for seventy-seven years during the reign of three sultans. When Aurangzeb conquered

Golkonda in 1687, it was still not complete. He was approached for sanction of funds for its completion. First, he made a caustic comment:

Kare duniya, kase tamaam naa karad
Harcheh geerad mukhtasir geerad

Meaning that no one can complete all the tasks of the world, so one should not take up more than one can accomplish. However, finally, he sanctioned the amount required for its completion. The mosque was thus completed in 1694.

Its hall is 67 meters long, 54 meters wide and 23 meters high. It is the largest mosque in south India and the second largest in the country after the Jami Masjid of Delhi.

It can accommodate about 5,000 worshippers at a time within its compound.[8]

At the south end of the spacious compound, is a gallery containing the graves of the five out of the seven Nizams and some members of their families. Opposite the gallery, there was a stone bench. It was believed that if any person sat on the bench, he would come back to the city. The bench was destroyed in the blast in the mosque in 2007.

Mecca Masjid Hyderabad, front view

THE LANGAR PROCESSION

Abdullah was accordingly brought up by his mother away from his father. Teachers were appointed for his proper education. Abdullah's young mother Hayat Bakhshi Begum supervised the arrangements and made sure that Abdullah left the palace before the return of his father, so that they would not come across each other. However, when only a few weeks remained for this prohibition to lift, the father and son ran into each other accidentally in the corridors of the palace. Soon thereafter, the Sultan was suddenly taken ill and, passed away within a month, in 1626.

Abdullah thus became the sultan of Golkonda at the tender age of twelve. His mother Hayat Bakhshi Begum became the regent. Because of her early indulgences for a son virtually without a father, Abdullah had grown up as somewhat of a spoilt boy.

Soon after his accession, Abdullah went on a ride on one of the two large elephants gifted to him by his father - called `Moorat'.

The river Musi was in spate. On approaching it, the elephant suddenly stopped and in spite of all the usual verbal commands of the mahout, it refused to go on to the bridge. The `mahout' then goaded it with the pointed iron hook. The elephant became angry, picked up the mahout with

Langar procession initiated since the time of Abdullah Qutb Shah every year on the fifth of Muharram

his trunk, and trampled him under its foot. Then it ran towards the jungle with the young sultan still sitting on it. Search parties were sent to locate and subdue the elephant but to no avail.

When informed about the incident, the sultan's mother, Hayat Bakhshi Begum, had small bags of food items and goatskin bags of water strung to the branches of trees ahead of the direction, which the elephant had taken so that Abdullah could pluck and eat them. The queen-mother prayed to God for her son's life and safe return. She vowed that if her son returned alive, she would place a gold chain on the head of the elephant and feed the poor.[9]

Seven days later the elephant returned, with Abdullah safe and sound. In accordance with her vow, Hayat Bakhshi Begum made Abdullah walk barefoot up to Hussaini Alam, got a chain of gold (called langar) weighing 384 oz. and free meals were also given to the poor. This practice continued even under the Nizams and a Langar procession was organised every year on the fifth of Muharram.

This practice was abolished in 1918.[10]

ADVENTURES OF A DIAMOND

The kingdom of Golkonda was known for its high quality diamonds. The world-famous *Koh-e-noor* (Mountain of Light) diamond was mined at Kallur in the Krishna River valley, probably in 1656 and it is said that originally its weight was 765 carats uncut. Mir Mohammad Sayyed came to Golkonda from Ardistan during the reign of Sultan Abdullah Qutb Shah of Golkonda (1626-1672). From a merchant, he rose to be Mir Jumla (prime minister) of Golkonda.

Koh-e-noor, now in London as part of the crown jewels of the British Monarch

He conquered Karnataka for Abdullah. This made him very rich and arrogant. He raised his own army and started defying the authority of his master. Abdullah took action against him by confiscating his property and arresting his son. He thereupon approached the Mughal

1. Kollur - Agra
2. Agra - Delhi
3. Delhi - Tehran
4. Tehran - Kabul
5. Kabul - Lahore
6. Lahore - London
ARCTIC OCEAN
RUSSIAN EMPIRE
SIBERIA
EUROPE
CHINESE EMPIRE
TURKESTAN
PERSIA
AFGHANISTAN
BELUCHISTAN
ARABIA
INDIA
TIBET
ARABIAN SEA
BAY OF BENGAL
SEA OF BENGAL
INDIAN OCEAN
EQUATOR
AFRICA
London
Agra
Haidarabad
Madras
Bombay
CALCUTTA
Rand, McNally & Co., Engr's., Chicago.

Emperor Shah Jahan and presented the magnificent Koh-e-noor to him. Shah Jahan was dazzled by its brilliance. The diamond was valued at ₹ 2,16,000 (£ 21,600). It seems to have been chipped before it was presented to Shah Jahan. Later it was entrusted to a Venetian named Bronzoni, and was so damaged and wasted in his hands that when Tavernier saw it in Aurangzeb's treasury in 1665 it weighed no more than 260½ English carats. In 1739, when Nadir Shah sacked Delhi, amongst his loot was the Koh-e-noor. The defeated Mughal Emperor, Bahadur Shah, had been warned against Nadir Shah's designs. He had therefore hidden it in his turban. Nadir Shah's spies told him about it. He then asked Bahadur Shah to exchange turbans with him as a gesture of friendship. He thus managed to get the diamond and carried it to Iran.

Thence it passed on to the kings of Kabul, and in 1809, Elphinstone saw it in the bracelet of King Shujah at Peshawar. Shah Shujah, the deposed ruler of Afghanistan, presented the Koh-e-noor to Maharaja Ranjit Singh, the ruler of Punjab, in 1814 to seek his

Travels and travails of Koh-e-noor *(Courtesy: Abhishek Patel)*

help in reclaiming his throne. The Maharaja sent it to his jewellers in Lahore for evaluation. The jewellers said that they had never seen anything like that before and so were unable to evaluate it. Ranjit Singh then asked Shah Shujah's wife about its value. She replied that if you throw a stone in all directions and up in the air, and then fill the space within with gold that would equal the value of the diamond.

In 1849, on the annexation of Punjab by the British, the seven-year old son and successor of Maharaja Ranjit Singh, Daleep Singh, was made to present it to Queen Victoria in London.

In 1852, Voorsanger recut it. Its present weight is 106½ English carats. It forms part of the jewels of the British monarch and is kept at the Tower of London. It is worn by the British monarch on coronation and other formal occasions[11].

A DOG ON THE THRONE

The Mughal Emperor Aurangzeb attacked Golkonda in 1687. For a long time, his army could not make any headway. One day Aurangzeb pulled up his generals for their lack of efficiency and the delay in reducing the fort. Cut to the quick by his observation, one night, one of his generals, Feroze Jung, planned a daring sortie on the fort. He took some of his soldiers close to the ramparts of the fort and while he stood below, the soldiers began to scale the walls with ropes. A pariah dog in the fort noticed the intruders and started barking. That woke up the garrison. The defenders killed many soldiers and repulsed the attack.

When the news of the episode was conveyed early next day to Sultan Tana Shah, he was very pleased with the dog that had saved the fort by his timely bark. He had the dog brought to him, honoured it with a silk coat, a studded collar, a gold chain, and made the dog sit on the throne along with him. Then, by way of a taunt to the unsuccessful Mughal general, he gave the dog the title of Feroze Jung.[12]

It was the only dog in the history of the world to have ever sat on a throne.

Aurangzeb's siege of the Golkonda Fort lasted eight long months and finally one of the generals whom he had bought by bribery opened the main gate of the fort, still called the Fateh Darwaza (Victory Gate). The Mughal army entered the fort after overcoming a brave and stiff resistance by the loyal General, Abdul Razzaq Lary. When the Mughal general, Ruhulla Khan, with a small contingent of soldiers went to arrest Tana Shah, he was at prayer. After the prayer, he came out and received his uninvited guests politely. An attendant came and announced that breakfast was ready. The sultan got up and invited the party to join him for the repast. Some Mughal officers tried to prevent him but their seniors pulled them back. Ruhulla Khan asked Tana Shah in surprise, 'Is this a time to eat?' Tana Shah replied calmly that this was his usual time for breakfast. Ruhulla said he understood that but what surprised him was how the sultan could feel any appetite after all that had happened. The sultan smiled and replied, 'Ups and downs come in one's life. I belonged to the royal family but spent fourteen years of my life as a mendicant. The Almighty raised me again from a humble position and made me a king. I have lived a full life. I must have been guilty of some sin that is why the Creator has made this happen. It is all the will of God. And everyone has to submit to it.[13]'

Thereafter, Tana Shah bade goodbye to the wailing women of his harem, mounted his horse, and accompanied his captors out of the fort.

Bala Hissar of Golkonda Fort
(Courtesy Abhishek Patel)

STRANGE LIFE OF TANA SHAH

The life of Tana Shah, the last Qutb Shahi ruler of Golkonda (1672-1687) reads like a fairy tale. His real name was Abul Hassan. He was distantly related to Abdullah Qutb Shah, the seventh sultan of the dynasty (1626-1672). He was therefore accommodated in the palace where he grew up. For some misdemeanour, he was expelled from the palace at the age of fourteen.

Having spent his infancy and adolescence in ease and comfort without having acquired any mental or physical wherewithal to earn a living, Hassan could not do a thing to support himself. On the advice of a friend he went to the monastery of a Sufi saint called Syed Shah Raziuddin, popularly known as Shah Raju Qattal. He was eighth in the line of Saint Khwaja Gesu Daraz Bande Nawaz of Gulbarga. He came to Hyderabad and set up his hospice on the west side of the Fateh Darwaza gate of the city (not the fort). He was an influential teacher of the Sufi doctrine and was believed to possess great spiritual powers. He was greatly revered by the people.[14] Sultan Abdullah Qutb Shah had become his disciple at an early age and, Shah Raju had a soft corner for him.

Raju took pity on the young boy expelled from the palace and accepted him as his disciple. Abul Hassan then became his errand boy and was constantly in and out of the cell in which Shah Raju spent most of his time in contemplation and meditation.

Abul Hassan had a good voice and sang well. He also had a certain innocence about him. Shah Raju therefore gave him the nickname of 'Tana Shah', which means a child saint. Having been brought up in the palace Abul Hassan was also of a delicate build and was often seen lost in reverie.

Abdullah had three daughters and no son. The eldest daughter was married to Prince Mohammad Sultan, son of Aurangzeb, after the treaty entered into between Aurangzeb as the Viceroy of the Deccan and Abdullah in 1656. As a consequence of this marriage the sultanate of Golkonda was to pass on to the Mughal prince on Abdullah's death. However, as fate would have it, for his having been on the wrong side of Aurangzeb in the war of succession to the Mughal throne, Mohammad Sultan was imprisoned by Aurangzeb and died in jail. Abdullah's second daughter was married to Nizamuddin Ahmed of Mecca. The youngest was engaged to Syed Sultan of Najaf. However, misunderstandings developed

Shah Raju Qattal

between the second son-in-law who was very powerful in the court and Syed Sultan. Because of that, the second son-in-law and a number of other members of the royal family opposed the proposed marriage of the third daughter of Abdullah to Syed Sultan.

Abdullah, in his confusion, went to consult his mentor, Shah Raju at his hospice. When it was announced that the Sultan was coming all the devotees who had gathered for the *darshan* of the saint quietly withdrew. Abdullah and Shah Raju met alone and Abdullah explained his predicament. Shah Raju asked him to come after three days.

After Abdullah had gone, the followers of Shah Raju came back to sit at his feet. Thereafter Tana Shah also scampered into his presence. Thereupon Shah Raju remarked involuntarily, 'Lo! One king goeth and the other cometh.' The audience laughed at this joke on Tana Shah.

At the palace, preparations for the marriage of the youngest daughter of the Sultan were going on. The prospective groom, Syed Sultan, was also getting ready to lead his wedding procession.

At the monastery, Shah Raju told Tana Shah teasingly, 'We shall get you married soon. Let us go through your wedding ceremonies[15].'

A bewildered Tana Shah submitted to the seemingly eccentric orders of his master. On

Portrait of Abul Hasan

the third day a messenger came from Abdullah asking for an appointment with the saint. Shah Raju told him that the Sultan was welcome and that he should bring with him appropriate dresses and gifts for a bridegroom, and a spare horse. When Abdullah came to the monastery accordingly, Shah Raju got hold of Tana Shah and presenting him to Abdullah, said, 'This is the groom. Take him to be your son-in-law.' Tana Shah was taken to the palace, given a good scrubbing and bath, doused with scents, decked in jewellery and in no time was made into a royal groom.

Poor Syed Sultan was waiting for the signal to start the wedding procession, but that signal never came. The switch of grooms was made at the last minute and instead of Syed Sultan, Tana Shah became the last son-in-law of Sultan Abdullah.

Syed Sultan fled from Golkonda and went to Aurangzeb. The Mughal Emperor laughed at this tragi-comedy and said, 'Never mind. We will get you married to the daughter of Mir Jumla.'

Tana Shah had spent fourteen years in the palace, the same period in the hospice of Shah Raju and now he was ready for the third phase of his life.

Abdullah died in 1672. Tana Shah who was very popular with the nobles was made the next ruler of Golkonda.

In 1687, Aurangzeb attacked Golkonda, defeated Tana Shah, and sent him as prisoner to Aurangabad. Tana Shah had ruled for fourteen years. The next fourteen years he spent in jail before his death. As it happened, Tana Shah's life was divided into roughly four spells of fourteen years each, the first in the palace, the next in the monastery of Shah Raju, the third as the sultan of Golkonda, and the last in prison [16].

THE ASAF JAHI DYNASTY

		Born	Period of Rule
1.	Qamaruddin Khan Asaf Jah I	1671	1720-48
2*	Ahmed Ali Khan Nasir Jung	1712	1748-50
3*	Hidayat Mohiuddin Khan Muzaffar Jung	-	1750-51
4*	Mohammed Khan Salabat Jung	1718	1751-62
5	Nizam Ali Khan Asaf Jah II	1734	1762-1803
6	Akbar Ali Khan Sikander Jah Asaf Jah III	1768	1803-29
7	Farkhonda Ali Khan Nasir-ud-Dowlah Asaf Jah IV	1794	1829-57
8	Tahniat Ali Khan Afzal-ud-Dowlah Asaf Jah V	1827	1857-69
9	Mehboob Ali Khan Asaf Jah VI	1866	1869-1911
10	Osman Ali Khan Asaf Jah VII	1886	1911-48

*These three rulers are not enumerated in the serial order of the Asaf Jahs because they were not granted the title of Asaf Jah.

AURANGZEB'S TOUR OF BHAGNAGAR

After his conquest of Golkonda, Aurangzeb went round the city of Bhagnagar. He did the tour on horseback escorted by a Qutb Shahi noble, Nemat Ali Khan.

The Emperor pulled up his horse near a palace, looked up, and exclaimed in wonder, 'It is a very, very tall building!'

Obviously, Aurangzeb had not seen such a tall palace. It confirmed the testimony of foreign visitors and chroniclers who had said that Bhagnagar was bigger and better than the Mughal cities of Agra and Lahore. The palace he was seeing had seven storeys.

'It is Dad Mahal (Palace of Justice), Your Majesty,' explained the escort.

Aurangzeb commented satirically, 'Rather say *Shaddad* Mahal.'

Shaddad was a Persian tyrant and so there was an implied denunciation of the vanquished enemy.

The loyal and self-respecting Qutb Shahi noble replied coolly, 'Sire, only those who are high-minded can build high-rise buildings.'

The interior of Bashir Bagh Palace

The victorious Emperor was rendered speechless by the allusion.

The tour was terminated abruptly[17].

Aurangzeb's son, Prince Azam, who was appointed as the governor of the conquered territory wrote to his father asking for increase in his allowance. Aurangzeb asked him to shift to one of the Qutb Shahi palaces. He wrote back saying, 'I won't be able to afford even their lighting expenses!'

Aurangzeb
(Courtesy: Abhishek Patel)

THE SEVEN KULCHAS

The sultanate of Golkonda was conquered by Aurangzeb in 1687 and made a part of the Deccan province of the Mughals. Mir Qamaruddin was appointed the governor of the Deccan in 1724. Since he held the office of 'Nizam-ul-Mulk', (prime minster) he came to be referred to as the Nizam. He was a remarkable man and was rated highly for his competence and self-respect. He was given the title of Asaf Jah after a minister of the biblical king Solomon who was known for his sagacity. The dynasty founded by him was thus called Asaf Jahi and it ruled from 1724 to 1948.

While on a shikar during his journey to the Deccan, he is said to have lost his way in a jungle. Thirsty, hungry and woebegone, he approached a hermit called Shah Inayat for some food and water. All that the saint could offer him was dry baked bread, called *kulcha,* and plain water. The exhausted noble had his fill and in spite of the hermit's insistence, could eat no more than seven loaves. Thereupon the hermit blessed him and remarked, 'My son you have eaten seven kulchas. Your dynasty will rule for seven generations.'

The flag of the Nizams had a circle in the centre and people said that it was the symbol of the kulcha. It is interesting to note that the first Nizam himself contradicted the theory saying, 'It does not represent a kulcha. My name is Qamar which means the Moon and so the emblem represents the Moon.'[18] It is even more interesting to note that despite his contradiction, his successors too continued to believe the story. There is a file in the State archives of Andhra Pradesh, which shows that the sixth Nizam approved the design of his flag in 1899 with a minute, 'It is good and proper. The small kulcha in the centre is not necessary. It should be replaced (with Nizam-ul-Mulk Asaf Jah), because the big white circle is the kulcha.'

As it happened, the Asaf Jahi dynasty did last seven generations. Though in fact there were ten Nizams, only seven are counted as member of the 'Asaf Jahi' dynasty. The title of 'Asaf Jah' was not conferred upon the second, third and fourth Nizams who ruled during 1748-1762 and spent all their time in internecine warfare. When the fifth Nizam, Mir Nizam Ali Khan, ascended the masnad in 1762, he was given the title and so became Asaf Jah II. It ended with the end of the rule of Mir Osman Ali Khan in 1948 when Hyderabad was integrated with India. On his death in 1967, his grandson Mukarram Jah inherited the title but in 1971, all titles were abolished. In any case, he was not a ruler though he held a private ceremony of accession.

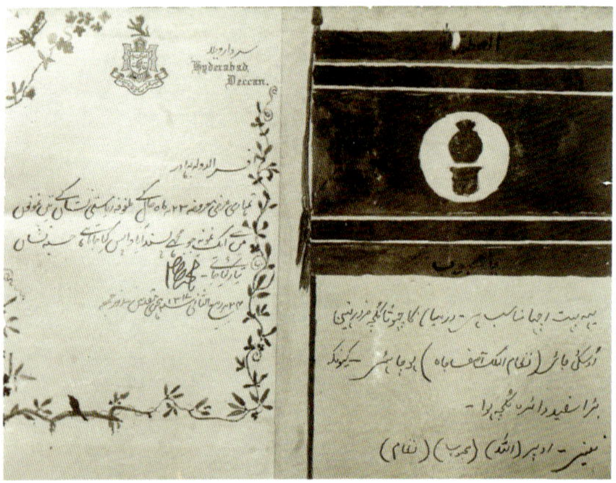

Hyderabad
Deccan.

The first Nizam also recorded in his will that he was leaving enough wealth to last seven generations.[19] In fact, that has so far lasted ten generations and one does not know how much longer it will go.

Sixth Nizam's Firman on the design of the flag
(Courtesy: Abhishek Patel)

A RESIDENT'S ROMANCE

The first British Resident was appointed to Hyderabad in 1779. James Kirkpatrick was the sixth Resident and served from 1798 to 1805.

The Resident used to stay in a garden-house of one of the Nizam's noblemen, Nawab Shamsher Jung. Kirkpatrick also occupied the same house for some time. However, after the Nizam signed the Treaty of Subsidiary Alliance in 1798 surrendering his sovereignty, Kirkpatrick became very powerful and so decided to build for himself a residence reflecting his new status as a representative of the supreme power in India. He sounded out the dewan, Arastu Jah, about the allotment of a suitable piece of land for the purpose. Arastu Jah saw no objection in the proposal and told the Resident to locate a site and get a sketch-map

The Residency

prepared to get the Nizam's approval. Separately, he secured the Nizam's concurrence to the proposal in principle.

However, when the Nizam saw the sketch-plan, he took one look at it and threw it away in horror. Kirkpatrick was crestfallen. He asked the dewan reason for this summary rejection.[20]

The dewan simply laughed, 'Resident Bahadur,' he chided the Englishman in good humour, 'you made the plan on a paper so large that it seemed to equal the size of His Highness's dominions. How could he agree to part with that?' Kirkpatrick, on hearing the reason, joined the dewan in laughter.

Obviously, the Nizam was not familiar with the principle of scale.

The Resident sought another audience and this time reduced the scale and got the sketch-plan for the same extent of sixty-four acres prepared on a piece of paper about the size of a visiting card. This time the Nizam readily agreed. Kirkpatrick then took up the project of building the Residency on the north side of the River Musi in 1800.

The building constructed was so grand that on a visit to Hyderabad in 1817, Sir John Malcolm wrote to Mrs Clive, the wife of the governor of Madras, that it was better than the Government House of

Khairunissa

Madras and, in splendour, next only to the Governor-General's House in Calcutta.[21]

The furniture for the Residency came from Carlton House in London. That was the residence of the Prince Regent and he wanted to dispose of his furniture. The Directors of the East India Company required some political concession and so they purchased the old furniture at the price wanted by the Prince. Incidentally, the Nizam paid for that, and met the expenditure for the maintenance of the Residency.

Kirkpatrick enjoyed his new abode. The Nizam granted him an Indian title - Hashmat Jung Bahadur - and it was only appropriate that he should adopt some of the ways enjoined by his new oriental knighthood. Accordingly, the young sahib acquired a mistress who stayed not far from the Residency.

Soon thereafter, Kirkpatrick married a Muslim girl called Khairunissa Begum who was distantly related to Mir Alam. The marriage was celebrated according to Islamic rites and Kirkpatrick wore the dress of a Muslim groom. However, Mir Alam, needled by the dewan, Arastu Jah, complained to the Governor-General about the wedding and the embarrassment which it might cause to the Nizam's Government, the British, and their mutual relationship.

James Kirkpatrick

The Governor-General ordered an inquiry into the case but thanks to Kirkpatrick's manipulation, a favourable report was sent to the Governor-General. Kirkpatrick also had a letter sent by Khairunissa's mother to the Governor-General testifying that the marriage was performed with her consent and blessing.[22]

The Nizam also issued a statement in favour of the Resident. The complaint was withdrawn and the complainant apologised.

Kirkpatrick built an annex for Khairunissa and named it *Rang Mahal.* Khairunissa gave birth to two lovely children – a boy, and a girl, in that order. In 1803, both children were sent to England for education. The boy died there, but the girl, Catherine, grew up and married into a good English family. She became known for her beauty and wit and was the first sweetheart of the great writer Carlyle, who immortalised her as Blumhilde in his novel *Sartor Resartus* published in 1836.

In 1805, Kirkpatrick suddenly fell ill. He was advised a change of air and rest. He left for Calcutta for consultations with the Governor-General. When his boat reached Calcutta, his illness took a turn for the worse and he died when he was barely forty-one. His marriage had lasted only six years.

A mob attacked the Residency during the mutiny of 1857, but it was beaten back.

The Residency now houses the University College for Women. Its ballroom is used for meetings of the general body of the students. The *Rang Mahal* is converted into Physics Laboratory.

CYPRESS OF GRACE

Chanda belonged to a good family of Gujarat which had fallen on evil days on the death of her grandfather. Her grandmother migrated to Rajasthan and taught singing and dancing to her daughters. Her daughter, in turn, passing through further hardships, came to Hyderabad during the rule of the Second Nizam, Mir Nizam Ali Khan, (1762-1803). Born in 1777, Chanda was adopted by the Nizam's childless dewan, Syed Lashkar Khan Rukun-ud-Dowlah (1765-1775}. Besides singing and dancing, she studied history and poetry and was a good rider with proficiency in arms.

She was a rare combination of beauty and brains. Her ready wit and charm made her a darling of the Second Nizam. He took her along on his military campaigns to Pangal and Nirmal and conferred on her the title of *Mah Laqa* (Moon-faced). She was free to attend the Nizam's durbar and to render advice to him. Two successive dewans of two Nizams – Arastu Jah (1797-1804) and Mir Alam (1804-08) were stricken by her. She is credited for having played a crucial rule in the appointment of Chandu Lal as dewan in 1832.

A popular story about her ready wit is that once while going in her palanquin a small *paandan* (a case for betel nut and betel-leaves) fell out on

Mah Laqa Bai Chanda

the ground. A young man remarked loudly, 'Mah Laqa's egg has fallen.' She retorted, 'What a marvel! As soon as it fell and broke, it has started crowing.'

A noble, Raja Rambha Rao, published her anthology of poems in 1798 making her the first female published poet of Urdu in India. It contained 125 ghazals of five couplets each. All of them, except four, end in praise of Ali and a plea for some favour from him. Two poems are in praise of the Second Nizam, and two of the dewan, Arastu Jah. In one of the poems about Arastu Jah, she thanks him for his favours including the grant of an elephant. She then requests him for the grant of a *jagir*.

In her odes to Ali, she uses most of his other names like Hyder, Murtuza and Maula. Her poems are in simple language. She writes about seasons

Tomb of Mah Laqa Bai Chanda *(Courtesy: Abhishek Patel)*

and on her own birthday. Some of them are marked by a rare boldness for a woman, like the following couplet:

Ham jo shab ko us shokh ke paale pade,
Dil to jaataa hi rahaa ab jaan ke paale pade
(Unexpectedly entrapped by him last night
Heart lost already, my life too was imperilled.)

She presented a copy of her book to Captain John Malcolm after her dance in Mir Alam's house in 1799. She also commissioned a book on the history of Hyderabad titled *Mah Nama* after her name. After her retirement, she set up a *taifa* – a centre for coaching young girls in music and dance. Some of the famous courtesans and dancers of later generations came from there. She had extensive jagirs and died a rich woman known for her charity in 1824.

She was buried in a tomb built by herself near the dargah of Maula Ali. Her epitaph in Persian describes her as 'cypress of the garden of grace and rose bush of the grove of coquetry, an ardent follower of Hyder and a supplicant of Panjtan.[23]' That attests to her Shia faith.

LAL BAZAAR

The Second Nizam signed the Treaty of Subsidiary Alliance with the East India Company in 1798. Under the terms of the treaty, six battalions of the Company's army led by Colonel Lang arrived at Hyderabad. They were stationed on the northeast of the Hussain Sagar Lake. They constituted the Subsidiary Force for the protection of the Nizam and his state. The encampment grew into the Secunderabad cantonment.

There was a prohibition against the marriage of young British soldiers sent to India. Such enforced celibacy led to the acquisition of Indian mistresses or liaisons with prostitutes. Soliciting in public was strictly forbidden in cantonments. A designated area was provided for the sexual gratification of the troops. Red jacket was the uniform of the British soldiers. It was translated into Hindustani, as '*Lal Kurti*'. Therefore, the designated area came to be known as 'Lal Bazaar'.

The women for this market were carefully selected by the cantonment authorities. They were required to register with the regimental authorities and were given a printed ticket in a prescribed form. They were medically examined every month and the results were recorded on the ticket. A matron ensured that the prostitutes were healthy. Those who were infected

vodafone

with VD were either expelled or sent to selected hospitals for treatment till they were certified as cured. Such hospitals were called 'Lock Hospitals' after the pattern in England. Soldiers infected with VD were also treated there. Cantonments committees made rules for the maintenance of the houses of the prostitutes in a state of cleanliness and for the prostitutes to be kept free of communicable diseases. Financial help was also offered to the women from the cantonment funds to buy furniture and other accessories for the comfort of their clients. These women also followed the regiment on its march and separate tents were provided for them at the new site. Army men had to pay a graded monthly charge according to their rank for the expenditure involved in the treatment of these women and the infected soldiers. It varied from one rupee a month from a sergeant to four annas from a private. The city of Hyderabad was strictly out of bounds for the British soldiers and those caught violating the ban were court-martialled.

In 1844 Captain Morgan, the superintendent of police of Secunderabad,

Lal Bazaar, Secunderabad, now *(Courtsey: Abhishek Patel)*

imposed a tax of two annas per month on every dancing girl and prostitute. The money was to be paid to a matron, who dispensed the required medicine to a needy prostitute. If she received soldiers before having been cured, she was 'most severely punished'. If the matron connived at any concealment of infection, she too was punished. In 1848, Brigadier J. P. James, commander of the cantonment cancelled these orders because he learnt that some matrons extorted money from respectable women under the threat of summoning them for examination. However, in 1855, his successor restored the old system. He set aside a ward in the civil hospital where the police brought women for examination and treatment. It was justified as a benign coercion against the spread of infection.

The system of Lock hospitals was first adopted in Chennai in 1805. They were closed in 1830 and reopened in 1864. A drawing published in *The Sentinel*, a weekly moralistic journal published by the Quaker, Alfred Dyer, in 1888 shows seventy-five cantonment stations where 'State-licensed harlotry was established by the British government in the Indian Empire.' Alongside is a plan of the Bareilly cantonment, typical of all cantonments where the tents of the prostitutes were pitched closer to those of the soldiers than the church. Finally bowing to moral pressure of public-spirited men, 'the shrieking sisterhood', and missionaries, they were abolished in principle in 1888 and in practice by 1894, only to be revived in 1897. Thus, it will be seen that formally or informally the system continued.[24]

Every cantonment under the British followed this pattern and even now has a Lal Bazaar. Today, Lal Bazaar is a thriving market selling army stores and supplies, as well as general merchandise. However, neither the businessmen, nor the shoppers, nor even the residents know the origin of its name.

A COVETED RENDEZVOUS

According to the Subsidiary Alliance with the East India Company signed in 1798, the Nizam surrendered his sovereignty to the Company. In exchange the Company undertook to station a military force to ensure the safety of his person and his state.

With the landing of the army according to the Treaty of 1798, India's first cantonment was born at Secunderabad.

For the officers of army the Secunderabad Public Rooms was set up to the north of the Parade Ground. The building was cruciform with three wings. One wing was a library, and another, a dining and luncheon saloon. The third wing was a theatre gifted to the Public Rooms by Nawab Ghalib Jung, an Arab noble.

A large area of Secunderabad was a part of the estate of Sir Salar Jung, the illustrious prime minister of Hyderabad from 1853 to 1883. He had a country house, which he gifted to the army for its use as a club in 1878.

The name of Secunderabad Public Rooms was then changed to Secunderabad Garrison Club, and later to Secunderabad Gymkhana Club. After the acquisition of some more land, it was given the name of the United Services Club in 1888. A 'splendid library', a ballroom, and a gymkhana were the core of the club. A Golf Club at Bolarum and a Sailing Club on the north-eastern end of the Hussain Sagar Lake were also attached to it. A military band played in the gardens opposite the Club three times a week, and periodically, the massed bands of the garrison entertained the public with choice programmes.

The all-white Club admitted all civil and military officers of the British Government stationed in Secunderabad, Bolarum, and Chaderghat (the habitation around the Hyderabad Residency outside the walled city of Hyderabad). Non-officials were balloted for an honorary membership. In 1898, the Club had 221 members. In 1903, it was given the present name of Secunderabad Club. The membership was also opened to 'those Indians who were deemed to be gentlemen of culture and position, irrespective of caste and creed, and members of nobility, businessmen of repute and gazetted officers of the State'. All the messes of the armed forces are automatically members of the club.

Mary Margaret Kaye (1908-2004) painted the murals in the Mixed Lounge. She was a novelist, dramatist, painter, and illustrator. She earned worldwide renown for her best-selling novel, *The Far Pavilions*, published in 1978. Her father, Sir Cecil Kaye, was a distinguished member of the Indian Civil Service who died in 1935. She was born in India and married an

Secunderabad Club

army officer who retired as a general of the British army. The murals were painted sometime between 1926 and 1935 when she was with her father in India. They depict English pastoral scenes in the Art Nouveau (New Art) style of painting.

Towards the end of the 20th Century, the murals started flaking. The hall also needed renovation due to seepage. This work was done by Kasim Ali Khan, an interior designer who also later designed the restructuring of the building of the Salar Jung Museum. Sanjay Ashtaputre, a painter, did the restoration work of the frescoes by M.M. Kaye. The original fresco was executed in egg tempera while the restoration was done in plastic emulsion.

The library was the next to be renovated. Apart from improving the get up, and providing air-conditioning in the main reading room, a mezzanine floor was added for reference books and Internet for which a separate cabin with eight computers was provided. A glass wall on the north provided a view of the swimming pools - a pleasant sight. The library has now 47,000 books and it subscribes to about hundred magazines and periodicals.

The prize feature of the Club library - and indeed of the Club - is the thirty-one volumes comprising 325 plates of Birds of Asia by John Gould (1804-1881). He was a gardener's son and grew up without any formal education to follow his father's profession. He had 350 volumes comprising 530 plates printed during 1850 to 1883. His wife, Elizabeth, who died in 1841, did most of the lithographs. They were lying in the library in a neglected condition and were about to be discarded when they came to the notice of Aasheesh Pittie, a keen bird watcher. He estimated that they would be worth about three crore rupees in the international market. They were immediately moved to a fireproof safe with two keys. One key is kept with the President and the other with the Secretary of the Club. They are aired once every three months. I had a view of these along with the late Siraj Taher, President of the Bird Watchers' Society of Andhra Pradesh. This society was established in 1983. The safe also contains a volume of *The Venomous Snakes of the Indian Peninsula* by Joseph Fayrer (1824-1907). Fayrer was an officer in the Indian Medical Service and honorary physician to Queen Victoria. The book, published in 1872, is very valuable.

In 2008 the old dining hall, having become structurally weak, was pulled down. Next year a sumptuous dining hall emerged in its place. Yeshwant Ramamurthy, a well-known architect and interior designer who was commissioned to design and construct the new dining hall, says that the inspiration for the artistic elements came largely from the art noveau style of painting and interiors. The furniture, stained glass, jacquard design for the drapery and upholstery weave are in the art noveau tradition. The customised wallpaper motif incorporates the club emblem. The old chandeliers were reconditioned and installed in a high vaulted ceiling. Painters were specially commissioned to create the two murals depicting colonial country life in Kaye's style. On the north wall is the Maypole Dance and the opposite wall depicts a picnic. Rajshekhar and Murali painted these murals. Adjoining the Dining Hall, a new Committee Chamber was added. On the west wall, a mural of the Club building was done in fibreglass by Bhumiraj. It gives the impression of plaster of Paris. Old and rare pictures of the club and Secunderabad adorn the other walls. They were specially procured from the British Library, London.[25]

The Club is now ranked as one of the top six in India and it enjoys affiliation with a number of clubs abroad. Its membership is highly coveted. The present admission fee is three lakh rupees and there is a waiting period of twenty-eight years. On completion of fifty years of membership, one becomes an honorary member and does not have to pay the monthly subscription.

THE THIRD NIZAM & THE TEMPLE

The Kayasths were the trusted civil servants of the Nizams. They had come with the First Nizam from the North and settled down in Hyderabad. They adopted the ways of the ruling elite and served as a bridge between the rulers and the subjects in all matters. They made good in their career and some of them rose to high civil and military positions, and even to nobility.

Nawab Sikandar Jah, the Third Nizam *(courtesy Salar Jung Museum)*

The first Kayasth to rise to nobility in the 19th Century was Bhavani Pershad. He was in charge of the salaries of the employees of the royal palaces. When he became prosperous, and was given the title of Raja, he decided to celebrate it by constructing a temple dedicated to Rama. The site was near Attapur about fifteen kilometres from the city off the road which leads from near the Nehru Zoological Park to Rajendra Nagar.

The story goes that the idol of Rama installed there was originally commissioned by Raja Som Bhopal of Gadwal for his own temple. Gadwal was a Hindu *samasthan* or a tributary estate in Raichur district of the old Hyderabad State. While the idol was being sculpted, the Raja had a dream in which he was told to retrieve an idol from the bottom of a well and instal it in the temple.

Ram Bagh Temple *(Courtesy: Abhishek Patel)*

At the same time, Raja Bhavani Pershad also dreamt of the idol commissioned by Raja Som Bhopal. He told the latter about his dream and made a request for the gift of the idol for his temple. Som Bhopal readily obliged since in his own temple, he had installed the idol, which he had retrieved from the bottom of the well.

When the temple was ready, Raja Bhavani Pershad invited the Third Nizam, Nawab Sikandar Jah (1803-29), to perform the ceremony of the installation of the idols of Rama, Sita, and Lakshmana. The Nizam agreed and the ceremony was performed in 1812.

Not only that, the Nizam also granted a jagir for the maintenance of the temple and sanctioned regular payment for its maintenance, including salaries to persons who looked after the temple.

Ram Bagh temple inner sanctum *(Courtesy: Abhishek Patel)*

The State Archives of Andhra Pradesh contains two documents relating to this temple. One is from *Daftar-e-Istifa* dated sixth Rabi-ul-Awwal, 1231 Hijri corresponding to 1816 AD. This sanctions a daily grant of two rupees to the persons who looked after the temple. The other is in favour of Raja Bhavani Pershad and is for the amount of ₹ 2,093, eight annas and four pice to meet the expenditure for the maintenance of the temple.[26] The priest for the temple was brought from Kerala.

From then on a regular annual 'yatra' takes place there on the Rama Navami day.

It is both surprising and inspiring that a Hindu temple should have been inaugurated by a Muslim. This did not 'contaminate' the faith of either.

This and similar acts reinforced the spirit of tolerance and communal harmony bequeathed to the city by its founder, the poet-king Mohammad Quli Qutb Shah (1580-1611) who, in one of his poems had said:

Kufr reet kya hor Islam reet
Har ik reet mein hai ishq ka raz.[27]
(What is paganism and what Islam?
The secret of all religions is love.)

CHANGE OF THE DURBAR PROTOCOL

The Nizams never declared their independence of the Mughal emperor. It was the British who forced the Fifth Nizam Afzal-ud-Dowlah to discard the nominal subservience to the Mughal Emperor who had been dethroned and exiled to Burma in 1858. This was done by striking coins in the Nizam's name and having his name replace that of the emperor in the Friday '*khutba*' in mosques. It was ironical that by then the Nizam had in fact become subservient to the British.

Mehboob Ali Khan, the Sixth Nizam
(Courtesy: Abhishek Patel)

In that regard, it was the accession of the Sixth Nizam in 1869, which turned out to be a watershed. That, in turn, was due to the fortuitous fact that the Nizam, Mehboob Ali Khan, happened to be less than three years old when he ascended the 'masnad' of Hyderabad. He was led to it, held by hand on each side by the prime minister, Salar Jung I, and the co-regent, the Paigah Rafiuddin.

The Resident, C.B. Saunders, objected that prior permission of the viceroy had not been obtained for the installation of the Nizam. He was told that such permission was not required.

Willy-nilly he had to accept the position. Until then, in his durbars, while the Nizam sat on his masnad, all the nobles including the Resident and his officers sat barefoot on the floor without any headgear.

However, for the Installation Durbar of the toddler Nizam, the Resident insisted that he and his officers would come with their shoes on and that they would sit on chairs and not on the floor. The co-regents and their advisors thought it prudent not to make an issue of it so that the question of accession was not put in jeopardy.

That was the first time when the British Resident and his officers sat on chairs on the right of the Nizam while the Indian nobles, following the age-old practice, sat on the floor. However, so as not to make them feel inferior, the Indian side of the floor was raised to the level of the chairs so that all the courtiers sat at the same level. Gradually, all the courtiers started following the new practice.[28]

In 1884 Mir Mehboob Ali attained majority. The viceroy, Lord Rippon came to Hyderabad to formally install him as the Nizam. The durbar held at that time reflected the new protocol.

EDUCATION OF THE SIXTH NIZAM

We have seen how the Second Nizam had shown an amusing lack of knowledge of the principle of scale while dealing with the case of the grant of land for the Residency. The British therefore wanted the child Nizam to be educated on modern lines. However, the nobility wanted to continue with the traditional system. After much discussion, a compromise was arrived at.

The Sixth Nizam with Captain Clerk

An Englishman, Captain Clerk, was appointed superintendent of education. A group of moulvis under him provided traditional religious education. To create a proper teaching atmosphere, a 'class' was constituted comprising sons of the dewan, Salar Jung, Paigah nobles, Kishen Pershad and some others. The teachers had to be extremely respectful to the child

Nizam. After all other pupils had arrived, an Indian teacher Mustakim Jung would go with folded hands to invite the eight-year old Nizam to the class.

The child that he was, Mehboob did not want to study and would run away to the palace. The teacher would run after him with folded hands entreating him to come to the class. If during the chase, Mehboob entered the *zenana* (female quarters), the teacher had to wait outside with folded hands. Sometimes it took quite a while to persuade him to come to the class because the sympathies of entire *zenana* lay with the young boy. The teacher waited outside with folded hands.

Agha Mirza Beg, a grandson of Mirza Ghalib was already teaching the dewan's sons. He was asked to assist Clerk. Mehboob asked him how the English language sounded like?

Beg said, 'I pray for your long life and prosperity'. On hearing that sentence Mehboob got up and walked away.

The next day, Beg brought a book with pictures and short stories. He read one lesson in English and then explained it in Urdu. The class was over.

The English alphabet followed from the next day on.

The royal student was punished by proxy. If he was not attentive or could not do a sum, the teacher would pick up some other innocent student and give him a verbal lashing or even a bit of corporal punishment. Another teacher would then whisper to the Nizam to note what happened to a student if he did not pay attention to his lessons.[29]

With such a mix of two systems, Mehboob grew up into a man who was at home both in his own as well as the world of the British. He was the first Nizam start to conversing in English and wearing western dresses. The other nobles followed the Nizam and soon the upper crust of society started adopting western language, dress, and manners.

AN EXTRA NIGHT'S PLEASURE

Mehboob's penchant for the cup and women had become a cause of concern by the time he attained puberty. The Resident wanted him shifted away from Mahtab Mahal, one of the four palaces in the Chow Mahalla complex near Charminar because he did not want him to be in the women's quarters all the time. The dewan proposed that he shift to the Residency and the Resident move over to Bolarum. The move was vigorously opposed by the *zenana*. The overactive intriguers interpreted this as a design on the part of Sir Salar Jung to remove the young ruler from the city and thus, usurp all powers. As a compromise, he was shifted to the Mahtab Mahal.

A high wall separated the bachelor's quarters from the female attendant quarters. The bachelor's quarters were inhabited, besides Mehboob, by his companions mostly from his school days, like Laik Ali Khan and Saadat Ali Khan, the two sons of Salar Jung, Kishen Pershad and some others. Mehboob was allowed to spend a night in the women's quarters once a week. One evening Mehboob wanted to spend an extra night in the female quarters. This was no easy matter since special permission was required for that and the quarters were closely guarded.

Mehboob hit upon a clever idea. He asked Kishen Pershad to get hold of a ladder. That was placed against the wall adjoining the female quarters. Then Laik Ali, who was the strongest of all the young men, was asked to scale the wall and pull out one of the maidens from the other side. The *modus operandi* was to join three or four *dupattas,* long headscarves of women worn with *salwar kameez*, together, tie one of them around the waist of a girl and pull her up to the top of the wall. After she had rendered her services, she was lowered safely back into the compound by the same method.

The guards noticed the incident. They were in a fix. To report it would be to invite trouble; yet not to report it would be considered a grave dereliction of duty and would be visited by severe punishment. Finally, the matter was discreetly brought to the notice of Salar Jung. He sent a note to Raja Narender since Kishen Pershad was his grandson. The latter was faulted for procuring the ladder.

Kishen Pershad explained that he was duty-bound to carry out the orders of his ruler. Further, he explained that it was Laik Ali who had used the ladder for the impugned act. Raja Narender agreed with the explanation given by his grandson and told Salar Jung that he would have done likewise if he had received such orders from his sovereign.[30]

Nothing came out of the inquiry, but Mehboob did not like the fuss made about the incident, and it rankled.

WORLD'S LARGEST WARDROBE

By the close of the 19th Century, the anglicisation of the Nizam and his court was almost complete. In all matters, like dress, manners, household furniture, it was a mark of distinction to be westernised. The restrictions on social intercourse between the Indians and the Europeans were a thing of the past. People learnt English and travelled to Europe if they could afford it. The government also evolved a scheme of giving scholarship to meritorious students. English games and sports like cricket, polo and horseracing became popular amongst the wealthy classes. The pursuit of pleasure was always a pastime of the nobility. Now it took added forms. The dancing girls were still called on celebrations, but now there were also balls and it was a sign of accomplishment amongst the leading families for men to be able to lead in the wives and daughters of the British army at Secunderabad Cantonment in ballroom dancing. European brands replaced the indigenous wines.

The motor car made its appearance in the last decade of the century and of course, the Nizam was the one to acquire the first vehicle. Other nobles followed suit.

Mehboob Ali Khan was a vain, narcissistic young man fond of dressing well. He was the first Nizam to start wearing the western dress. He never wore the same dress twice. The result was that he came to have the largest wardrobe in the world. The entire right wing of his palace, 'Purani Haveli' with a length of 240 feet (73.15 metres) was full of clothes, shoes and other accessories. They took 124 almirahs – sixty-four in one ground row and sixty on the second row atop the first to accommodate them. In between the wardrobes in the lower row, there were some changing rooms. Most of the clothes were given away to make room for new ones. Today only the bare almirahs remain. One top hat in a box, two pairs of riding boots, a pair of pumps and one pair of straw slippers were all that was left of that fabulous collection when I visited it in 1991. I could see from

World's largest wardrobe
(Courtesy: Abhishek Patel)

the sole of the shoes that they could not have been worn more than once. The name of the London manufacturer was intact on the sole.

The wardrobe and the hand-operated lift to reach it still exist. In the hall next to it is the Silver Jubilee Museum of the Seventh Nizam.

Over a century has elapsed since the death of the once-only wearer of fabulous dresses – of both oriental and western style. However, the wardrobe and the hand-operated lift used to reach it still exist. While the lift is not in good shape, the wardrobe retains its original sheen and shape. The secret of that is that it was made of Burma teak. It is explained that Burma teak is impervious to termite attacks.

In the hall adjoining the wardrobe, a new museum has been opened based largely on the gifts the Seventh Nizam received on the silver jubilee of his rule celebrated in 1937 – a year later than due because of the death of King George V in 1936. It is called HEH the Nizam's Museum.

CHLOROFORM & THE SIXTH NIZAM

The Sixth Nizam, Mir Mehboob Ali Khan (1866-1911) was a popular ruler. There are numerous stories and legends about his indulgences and eccentricities. He claimed that he possessed the power to cure people of snakebite and that any victim could call him for help at any time of the day or night. Even today, you may see people at his grave in the Mecca Masjid offering floral tributes because someone in the family had been cured of snakebite by invoking his name – 'Mehboob Pasha *ki duhai*'.

He is also remembered for helping tackle the controversy concerning the use of chloroform as an aid to surgery. Chloroform was discovered in 1831 but was first used in 1847 by Dr James Simpson in Edinburgh. While hailing its advent, the medical men of London expressed a caution that its use posed a risk to the heart of the patient. The Edinburgh School, on the other hand, held that it was entirely safe for the heart and that the risk of its use was to respiration. If care was not taken of that aspect, it might cause a choking of the breath.

Surgeon-Major Edward Lawrie of Indian Medical Service was the principal of the Hyderabad Medical School and superintendent of Afzalgunj Hospital (now Osmania General Hospital) in 1885. He was also concurrently the chief medical officer of the British Residency and personal physician to the Nizam. He served in that capacity until 1901 when he retired. About 40,000 operations were performed in the Afzalgunj Hospital under his supervision by using chloroform as a general anaesthetic. Lawrie was a believer in the theory of Dr Simpson and was keen to prove its correctness. He persuaded the Nizam to pay for a scientific investigation into the controversy regarding the risk of the use of chloroform.

Accordingly, a commission comprising Lawrie and three of his colleagues was set up. They conducted numerous experiments on dogs which confirmed Simpson's theory, and publicised the results enthusiastically. *Lancet,* the renowned journal of the British Medical Association, pulled up Lawrie for rushing to conclusion on inadequate evidence. Thereupon, Lawrie, with the approval of the Nizam, announced that a second Commission would be set up. He invited the editor of the *Lancet* to nominate an expert of his choice to serve on the Commission. The Nizam invited him as a guest of the government and sanctioned a grant of 1,000 pounds sterling for his travel expenses.

The *Lancet* nominated Dr T.L. Brunton as its representative to serve on the Commission, which comprised, besides the members of the first Commission, three new members, one of whom was an Indian, Dr Rustomji Hakim. The Commission sat for three months and conducted in all, 600 experiments on different animals. So keen was the keenness of interest of the

Chloroform Commission 1889
(Courtesy: Abhishek Patel)

Surgeon-Major Edward Lawrie, Indian Medical Service *(Courtesy: Salar Jung Museum)*

Nizam in the project that on 29 November 1889, he himself visited the Afzalgunj Hospital and witnessed the administration of chloroform to three different animals – a goat, a horse and a monkey.

The second Commission confirmed the findings of the first Commission that it was the care of respiration and not of heart that was crucial in the administration of chloroform. These findings were published in the *Lancet* and, in its issue of 21 June 1890, its editor expressed the gratitude of the medical profession to Nizam Mehboob Ali Khan 'for the opportunity of scientific progress which his unbounded liberality has afforded.'

Later, Lawrie proceeded to London along with some of his distinguished students – Dr M.G. Naidu (husband of Sarojini Naidu), Dr Mohammed Abdul Ghani and Dr S. Malanna.

They demonstrated the Hyderabad Chloroform Technique in a London hospital on 25 May 1895.[31]

THE DEADLY MRS ANOPHELES

Son of a general in the Indian army, Ronald Ross was born in Uttar Pradesh in 1857. His heart lay in art, music and literature. However, to please his father he enrolled for medicine. Even as a student, he wrote a novel, stories, and a number of poems, and composed music. He also learnt Italian, German, and French and studied the great poets of those languages in the original.

On his first visit to India as a member of the Indian Medical Service, in 1881, Ross was struck by the stark poverty and poor health of the people at Chennai. He wrote a poem that concluded by asking:

> *Cannot the mind that made the engines make,*
> *A nobler life than this?*

In India, he served at a number of places like Chennai, Bengaluru, Vizianagaram, Quetta, Andamans and in Burma. After six years in India, he went to England on furlough, obtained a diploma in the then new subject of sanitation, and studied bacteriology. On return to India in 1890, he was sent to Bengaluru to tackle the cholera epidemic. He recommended a scheme of sanitation there in 1896 that was the first sanitation programme in India. He said that the work of a scavenger must precede that of the philosopher, and politicians!

He became aware of the problem of malaria in Bengaluru. The medical theory at that time was that malaria was caused by breathing the damp air of the marshes. Ross began his serious study of the subject while on a holiday in Coonoor and identified the two varieties of mosquitoes one of which – later identified as Anopheles – carried the parasite.

Ross integrated the isolated findings of Louis Pasteur, Robert Koch, Laveran, and Beauparthy to determine the process of transmission of malaria. He concentrated his efforts on the study of the parasite in the mosquito rather than in the patient.

Ross used to tempt his patients to be bitten by mosquitoes infected by malaria by paying them one rupee each. He would then let loose a swarm of mosquitoes (of which he always kept a bottle-full ready) into the mosquito net under which the patient was made to sleep. To tempt the mosquitoes, he would wet the bed and the net with water. Then he dissected the infected mosquitoes and examined them under a microscope.

His last experiment was on a patient called Hussein Khan. And it was the very last mosquito, a dappled Anopheles, which showed itself as the carrier of the malaria parasite. Ross thus established that the parasite was sucked in by the female Anopheles, incubated in its stomach for seven days or more, and brought up into its salivary glands in the mouth from where it was injected through its bite to other human beings. This great discovery of the process of the transmission of malaria was made on 20 August 1897 at Hyderabad. This led to the methods of control of the dreaded disease.

Sir Ronald Ross, pioneer in Malaria Eradication Research *(Courtesy: Abhishek Patel)*

For his monumental discovery, Ross was awarded the Nobel Prize for Medicine in 1902. He was knighted in 1911.

The Suez and the Panama canals were completed after getting rid of the mosquitoes from there. Mauritius, Greece, Cyprus, and Spain also implemented malaria control measures under his advice.

All his researches were carried on by him entirely at his own expense and despite obstructions from his superiors. Once his leave was not extended and he was posted back to his regiment where there were no facilities for research. That, however, did not deter him from his mission.

In his acceptance speech of the Nobel Prize he referred to 'the dingy little military hospital, old cracked microscope and the medicines bottles, which constituted all the laboratory and apparatus, which I possessed for the purposes of taking on one of the most redoubtable of scientific problems.' Sir Ronald Ross died full of glory in 1932.

Many countries of the world acknowledge the debt of gratitude to him. Malaria was a public health problem in more than ninety countries representing ninety percent of the world population.

In India it was a major killer till 1953 when a National Malaria Control Programme was launched followed by the National Malaria Eradication Programme in 1958. By 1965 the incidence came down from seventy-five million to 0.1 million cases. Later, however, it reemerged due to official laxity.

There is a ramshackle building near the airport. A road was named after him but the name was soon changed to 'Ministers Road'. In an ironic tribute to the memory of his work, swarms of mosquitoes inhabit his unpretentious laboratory tucked away near the old Begumpet airport![32]

THE SIXTH NIZAM & THE ARCHDUKE

No Nizam ever went out of India. Till the end of the 19th Century, even the prime minister of Hyderabad had to take permission of the Nizam to go out of the walled city of Hyderabad. However, the last two Nizams entertained a number of foreign dignitaries.

Prince Albert Victor visited Hyderabad in 1889. King George V while he was still Prince of Wales visited the State with his wife Mary in 1905. A special shikar trip was arranged for him. Another important visitor was the Archduke Franz Ferdinand of Austria in 1893. He was heir-apparent to the throne of Austria and his murder in Sarajevo triggered the First World War.

The Archduke kept a diary of his travels and it was published in Vienna in 1895. It contains an interesting account of Hyderabad and his tour. He notes shrewdly: 'The Nizam is a tributary prince supervised by an English Resident and a British garrison under the pretence of protecting him. Anti-British feelings are thus kept under control. He rules over 214,000 square kilometres and eleven and a half million inhabitants…'

About Mehboob's personality, he noted: 'The Nizam is twenty-eight years old, of small, lean stature, has a black sparse beard and long hair

The Sixth Nizam and the Archduke of Austria in a shooting match

reaching down to his shoulders; his face is yellowish, the small eyes are intelligent. Towards Europeans, he is reserved, even shy and very reticent. But vis-a-vis his subjects he is said to be able to behave very firmly. He is always dressed in European attire, usually in a black coat. The only thing he has retained of his indigenous costume is a turban-like cap of yellow cloth with a golden tassel (dastar). He never goes without this headgear. The Nizam seems to like the European dress and customs, in his own way, although in general he is not too fond of the Europeans which are understandable after the experiences he had with them.'

At the Nizam's palace, they sat down on 'two throne-like chairs which were placed adjacent to each-other. I and Kinsky did most of the talking ...

Asman Ghar Palace, Hyderabad

unfortunately without being able to incite the ruler out of his unshakeable reticence, since he limited himself to a saying "Yes" occasionally.'

The Nizam invited the Archduke to a shooting competition. The Archduke 'agreed reluctantly since the Nizam is known as the best sharpshooter in the whole country.'

First, several bottles were placed at a distance of thirty steps and clay balls the size of small apples were placed on their necks. They had to shoot the clay balls without hitting the bottle. The Nizam shot first and missed four clay balls. The Archduke followed and hit three out of four. Sportingly, the Nizam and his retinue burst into a loud applause.

Next to the bottles meant for the match, there were another sixteen bottles. With boosted confidence the Archduke undertook to shoot at all of them one after the other. He hit fifteen while the Nizam looked on in growing amazement. Then they had four shots each hitting one bottle with each shot. The result with tossed clay balls was similar.

Then came the most difficult part according to the Archduke. They had to shoot rupee coins flung high into air. Each of them had eight shots. The Nizam hit one, the guest was lucky to hit three though he had no experience of that. The Nizam was very sporting and showed his appreciation although it was the first time that he had been beaten at this game. 'I must admit that deep inside I felt as proud as a lion,' noted the Archduke.

Later, the Archduke visited the favourite summer resort of Asman Jah (prime minister 1884-94). In the courtyard, there were five chained tiger cubs approximately one year old. Asman Jah had shot the mother the year before and brought home the cubs. They had grown big, but were very cute. They played like little kittens. They were tame so that one could fondle them. To his delight, the prime minister presented two of them to the Archduke. 'I hope they will reach Vienna alive and safely,' wrote the Archduke in his diary.

Incidentally, the translator of the travelogue, Ms Al-Himrani checked the records of the Vienna Zoo and the keeper confirmed that two cubs had been donated to the zoo by the Archduke in 1893.

It is interesting to note that the account of this match in Hyderabad in Urdu showed the Nizam as the winner and the Archduke as a gracious loser![33]

NIZAM'S USTAD

The ideal ruler in Islam is a combination of a warrior and a poet. Since not every ruler could be a poet, it was quite common for them to appoint an *ustad* – a poetic preceptor – to teach them how to compose poetry, and if necessary, to ghost-write it for them.

Nawab Mirza Khan 'Dagh', the celebrated Urdu poet (1831-1905), was born in Delhi. He was educated in the Red Fort. After the Mutiny, he moved with his family to Rampur where he was treated with special consideration.

After the death of Nawab Kalbe Ali Khan, he moved to Hyderabad. Though he was greatly admired, he could not get any job. For ten long years, his one great wish was somehow to have an opportunity of an audience with the Nizam.

Meanwhile his renown spread all over the State. In the city, one special *mushaira* used to be held every month and in that, Dagh used to cast a spell on the audience with the recitation of his poems.

One day Maharaja Kishen Pershad, the prime minister, mentioned about him to the Nizam. The latter sent for him, and on hearing his poems, was swept off his feet. He was effusive in his praise. From then on Dagh

Nawab Mirza Khan 'Dagh' Dehlvi *(Courtesy: Abhishek Patel)*

was often invited to join the Nizam at dinner. He would stand for hours in front of the Nizam but did not get any job – not even a gift.

One day, the Nizam went for a hunt. There, in the jungle, all of a sudden, he thought of Dagh. He asked the prime minister, Kishen Pershad, to have Dagh fetched immediately.

Within two hours, Dagh stood with folded hands before the Nizam. On the evening of the second day, the Nizam was sitting resplendent on a chair in a sprawling field. All the courtiers and members of the staff were standing respectfully on either side. Some riders were giving a demonstration of their horsemanship. The Nizam was watching each of them with great interest. One refractory horse was giving a lot of trouble to his rider but the latter was also an expert. He sat on the back of the horse as a nail riveted to a piece of wood.

All of a sudden, the Nizam turned to Dagh and asked him, 'Dagh, have you ever done any riding?' Dagh replied with folded hands that in his youth, he had done so but years had gone by since then.

The Nizam said, 'Alright, show us your riding skills today.'

Dagh shivered at the thought, but had to obey.

On a signal from the Nizam, as if by a conspiracy, the same frisky horse was brought before Dagh. As soon as poor Dagh mounted it, the trainer cracked his whip on the beast. In an instant Dagh was somersaulting on the ground and the horse bolted away towards the jungle. The entire gathering was rolling with laughter. Dagh got up, dusted himself, and came and stood before the Nizam who was still convulsing with laughter. When he recovered, he addressed the crestfallen Dagh, 'You are a good rider. I appoint you as my head syce.' Dagh's heart sank, but according to etiquette, he bowed gratefully and salaamed the Nizam seven times. The Nizam then asked him, 'How long have you been in our State?'

'Ten years, *Ala Hazrat*.'

The Nizam turned to his prime minister and said, 'We appoint Dagh as the court-poet on a salary of one thousand rupees per month.'

'As His Highness pleases,' Kishen Pershad said, bowing.

'With retrospective effect. You understand?'

'Yes, Sire.'

'And,' added the ruler, 'his salary with arrears for the last ten years should be paid right away.'

The Maharaja said, 'Yes, My Lord,' in disbelief and retraced his steps. A dispatch rider was rushed with orders to the treasurer in the city for compliance. The Nizam then retired to his tent and the nobles in attendance swarmed round Dagh to congratulate him.

In those days, there was no paper money. So, the next day the whole city saw carts loaded with bags of silver coins carrying the arrears of ten years' salary of Dagh with police escort, arriving at Dagh's house on Abid Road. Dagh then embarked on a life of luxury.[34]

In one of his ghazals, he wrote:

Udate hain maze duniya ke hum ai Dagh ghar baithe
Deccan mein ab to Afzal Ganj apni aish manzil hai
(I enjoy myself sitting at home,
My abode is now in Afzal Ganj)

He died in 1905 and was laid to rest in Hyderabad.

THREE ECCENTRIC ORDERS

In the feudal state of Hyderabad, there were many practices, which today may seem rather odd and amusing. We have seen how Dagh was appointed as the poetic preceptor of the Sixth Nizam. Here are some more amusing orders.

Punishment of an Apprentice

In the 19th Century, it was customary for many persons to enrol themselves as 'candidates' for jobs in government departments for which they were qualified. However, due to lack of vacancy, they were not paid any salary. They had to work in an honorary capacity till a regular vacancy arose to which they could be appointed. Once such a candidate wrote a note on a file, which was misleading.

The prime minster, Salar Jung I, ordered that the author of the note should be fined ten rupees. It was submitted to him that since the 'candidate' did not get any salary he could not be fined.

The prime minister thereupon ordered that he should be appointed to some post with salary and the fine of ten rupees be deducted from his salary.

Enhanced Pension by Mistake

The Sixth Nizam, Mehboob Ali Khan was a very generous ruler. Once his personal attendant requested for superannuation because of old age and ill health. While granting the request, the Nizam ordered that he be paid a pension of eight rupees per month for life. In the draft order, due to a mistake, instead of the figure 8, the figure of 80 was written. When the Nizam was about to put his signature to the order, the clerk detected the mistake, apologised, and came forward to correct the figure. The Nizam stopped him and observed, 'If it was ordained that he would get this fortuitous benefit, how can you or I prevent it?' He then signed the order and the lucky attendant enjoyed the bounty till the end of his life.

Special Allowance for Beard

Rehman Khan was a Risaldar Major in the Third Lancers of the Hyderabad Army and worked in the private secretariat of Nawab Afsar Jung, Commander-in-Chief under the Sixth Nizam. He used to accompany Afsar Jung to the residence of the Sixth Nizam at Purani Haveli.

One day he was riding a horse at great speed within the premises of the palace. He sported a thick long beard, which swayed in the air because of the speed at which the horse was galloping. The Nizam watched this spectacle and was very impressed by the flowing beard. He ordered a special allowance of ten rupees a month for its maintenance. Rehman Khan received this allowance along with his pension till his death.[35]

A MAVERICK MINISTER

Nawab Shahab Jung was the minister for police under the Sixth Nizam, Mir Mehboob Ali Khan. He was a favourite of the Nizam and his mansion was close to the Nizam's palace, Purani Haveli. In the evening hundreds of candles and lamps would be lit up in the minister's mansion. There were two costly chandeliers in the drawing room, each with thirty-two lotuses engraved in gold and silver. They cast so much light that it looked like day. The reason for such lavish lighting was that Shahab Jung did all his work - receiving callers, granting interviews, instructing the managers of his estates only at night. The kotwal of police also briefed him and received his instructions at that time.

With throngs of petitioners, respondents, lawyers, job seekers, the atmosphere in the compound resembled a fair. Petty vendors opened stalls in the compound to cater to the needs of the people. The thing for which Shahab Jung became a legend was the relay of liveried attendants from his office room to the private apartments to meet his needs. If, for example, he asked for water, the order would be transmitted from mouth-to-mouth loudly from the minister's office till it reached the pantry. The cook would fill a silver tumbler with water, put it on a silver tray, and pass it on to the man next to him, announcing, 'Water, Sir.' This tray would then be relayed back with a loud declaration from each servant right up to the Nawab. The announcement was shrill enough to wake up the dozing lawyers.

After a while, Shahab Jung would ask for a paan. This time the demand would be relayed to the private apartments from where a lady would prepare the special paan and the servants would relay it back to the master. Demand for a cigar, or anything else would also be fulfilled similarly.

This commotion continued throughout the night.

Early one morning, the Nizam happened to come up to his terrace to enjoy the cool breeze. Suddenly, he heard the shrill announcement: 'Water, Sir' being repeated endlessly. The Nizam asked what the racket was all about. Nawab Shamsher Jung explained, '*Ala Hazrat*, Nawab Shahab Jung must have asked for water.' The Nizam just smiled and kept quiet.

Next day, the Nizam summoned Shahab Jung. 'Because of the commotion from your mansion throughout the night, I cannot sleep. Why don't you shift your residence?' asked the ruler.

Shahab Jung bowed and submitted with folded hands, 'This slave has only one abode, Sire. If he leaves it, where will he find a shelter? My sovereign, on the other hand, has dozens of palaces. If this servant of His Highness were in that situation, he would have instantly complied with the royal orders.'

Nawab Shahab Jung

The Nizam caught the hint and kept quiet.

Once a committee of the nobles of the state was slated for a meeting under the Nizam. Unable to go, he asked his chief secretary, Moulvi Ahmed Hussain, to deputise for him. The Maulvi informed all members of the committee about the Nizam's orders and proceeded to conduct the meeting.

Thereupon Nawab Shahab Jung got up and said it was inconceivable that a paid servant of the State should preside over a committee of nobles. Turning to the chief secretary, he said, 'This committee comprises leading nobles of the State. You may be getting a salary of three thousand rupees but you are nevertheless an employee. You cannot therefore preside over this meeting.' The chief secretary protested that he was merely carrying out the orders of His Highness. Jung told him that he would answer the Nizam suitably but the chief secretary should withdraw.

The Nizam was incensed on hearing about the incident. He asked the delinquent Nawab in great anger, 'What audacity? You did not care for my orders and sent away my representative!'

The minister replied with folded hands, 'Your Highness, the committee comprised all the nobles of Hyderabad. How could this slave allow the indignity of letting a paid employee sit amongst them?'

The Nizam said, 'The nobles are all my creatures. I can put my shoe on anyone's head.'

The Nawab persisted, 'This humble servant is fully aware of that. But my sovereign, the only fit place for the blessed shoe is the head of Shahab Jung. Your Highness cannot place it anywhere else.'

The explanation pacified the Nizam. The Nawab returned home triumphant.

Once, for some infraction on the part of the police commissioner, the Nawab imposed a fine of one rupee on him. The Nizam, on coming to know about it, asked Shahab why he had done that when he knew that the police commissioner was his trusted employee and well-wisher. Shahab Jung said he would reconsider his orders.

Coming back to the office, he ordered, 'Half the fine remitted. Let him pay half-rupee.'

And the commissioner had to comply.

Shahab Jung's glory did not survive the accession of the Seventh Nizam. The story goes that some of the nobles showed reluctance to acknowledge the authority of the Nizam. He mentioned about this to Shahab Jung. The latter said not to worry. 'I will come to the court late tomorrow. Your Highness may rebuke me for that. That would serve as a warning to others.' When, the Nizam started mock reprimanding him, he really lost his temper and started using foul language. Nawab Shahab Jung felt so humiliated that he withdrew completely and never came out of his mansion. Having lived out his life in reclusion, he emerged from his mansion wrapped in a coffin and nobody could see his face.[36]

INDIA'S GREATEST LENSMAN

Deen Dayal was born in 1844 in a well-to-do Jain family of Sardhana near Meerut in Uttar Pradesh. After completing the lower subordinate course at the Roorkee Engineering College, he worked as a draughtsman in the princely state of Indore. He showed extraordinary skill in photography and came to the notice of the viceroy. He undertook a tour of the country to photograph monuments and published the photographs in his first album, *Views of India.*

That brought him instant recognition and he resigned his job. Deen Dayal once took a portrait of the wife of the viceroy, Lady Dufferin in which he made her look younger than she was. This reinforced his merit to become a favourite with the viceroy. In 1885, he came to Hyderabad with a letter of introduction from the viceroy, Lord

Dufferin, to the Sixth Nizam, Mehboob Ali Khan. The Nizam appointed him his State Photographer. The Nizam used to wear a special *ittar* (Indian scent) and after using the swabs, threw them away carelessly. Whenever Deen Dayal took any picture in which the Nizam figured, he used to dab the back side of the photo with one of the swabs. A surprised Nizam once told him, 'It is remarkable, Deen Dayal. You are able to bring out my scent also in my picture!' The Nizam was so impressed by the quality of his work that he conferred the title of Raja on him. Deen Dayal set up a studio in Secunderabad. It employed about fifty persons including some Europeans, as well as an Englishwoman for taking photos of purdah women. In 1887, Raja Deen Dayal received the Royal Warrant of Appointment as photographer to Queen Victoria – the only Indian ever to receive that honour.

The Archaeological Survey of India acquired 250 of his photographs of old monuments from him to undertake its restoration work. The Nizam's government utilised his services for its archaeology, public works, forest, revenue and registration and other departments. He thus contributed greatly to the preservation of the architectural heritage of India.

His versatile artistic competence was strongly reinforced by his methodical approach to his work. He catalogued meticulously all the pictures that he took. Deen Dayal won twelve international awards from different countries like USA, Italy, Spain, England and Japan. Today, his photographs are treasured all over the world. In India, the Indira Gandhi National Centre for the Arts, the Alkazi Foundation and some private persons have a comparatively small number of his photographs. Grief-stricken by the death of his wife and son, Deen Dayal died in Mumbai in 1905. His studio no longer exists but some of his descendants have their business in Hyderabad and Secunderabad.[37] One branch of the family continues to stay in a part of the ancestral house in Sardhana.

A RAJA & A HORSE

The Hindu estates in Hyderabd were called *samasthans*. They predated the Nizams and the Qutb Shahi dynasty and so were not under them. However, being very small, they paid tributes to them.[38] One such estate was Domkonda in the present Nizamabad District, about hundred kilometres north of Hyderabad. It was ruled by the Rajas of Kamineni dynasty of the Reddy community. This *samasthan* comprised a number of villages in two taluks of Kamareddy and Yellareddy. Its fort is still intact in parts and so are some of its beautifully carved buildings and the Siva Temple inside the fort.

Someshwer Rao was the Raja during the late 19th and early 20th Century. The Sixth Nizam, Mir Mehboob Ali Khan, liked him as a connoisseur of horses and often sought his help in selecting horses for his stable. The Raja never let slip any opportunity of acquiring horses of good breed.

Once a junior revenue officer of the area visited Domkonda on tour. He proudly rode into the presence of Raja Someshwer Rao inside the fort, on his pied charger called 'Ablaq' meaning black and white. Seeing the beautiful horse, Raja Someshwer Rao showered honours on the officer liberally and entertained him lavishly as his guest for a period longer than was usual.

The reason for such unusual warmth was that the Raja had fallen in love with 'Ablaq' and wanted to acquire it at any cost. He did not have such an animal in his stable, nor had seen such a wonder. Discreet hints were given to the officer, but he did not react. An attractive offer to buy the horse was made, but the owner of the horse did not accept it. Several schemes were considered, but none was found feasible.

Finally, the Raja took to the solution of the last resort. He took out his pistol, shot the recalcitrant official dead, had his body bundled into a gunnysack and thrown over the fort of the wall into the moat. The place is still marked and is pointed out by old timers.

When the news reached the Nizam in Hyderabad, he was furious that one of his trusted Rajas should have behaved in such a manner. He issued orders for the Raja to be brought to Hyderabad and kept under house arrest in the city. The Raja could not but obey the orders of the Nizam, but there was a small snag. The Raja did not have a house in Hyderabad where he could serve the sentence. To overcome this problem, a large house with several acres of land around it was quickly located and the Raja was lodged there. Negotiations went on for the purchase of the property for quite some time before the deal was finalised. After some time, the Raja was allowed to go back to his *samasthan* with strict instructions not to repeat such delinquency.

The place in Hyderabad that Raja Someshwer Rao thus acquired was later named 'Uma Bagh' after the name of his son Raja Umapathy Rao. That Uma Bagh, about ten acres in extent in the present Nampally area on the main road near the Railway Station, continued to be the peaceful residence of the siblings of the Kamineni Rajas of Domkonda till the late 1970s. Now it is a busy commercial area where the Medinova Hospital, Raghava Ratna Commercial Towers, Shalimar Garden Function Hall, etc, have sprung up. The erstwhile owners live in different parts of the city.[39]

A MULTIFACETED NOBLE

One of the most colourful and powerful nobles of Hyderabad was Maharaja Sir Kishen Pershad.

He traced his lineage to Raja Todar Mall, the revenue minister of the Mughal emperor, Akbar. He was the hereditary *peshkar,* next to the dewan, of Hyderabad. He was a class-fellow of the Sixth Nizam, who appointed him minister for military affairs in 1895, and prime minister in 1900.

In 1911 when Mir Osman Ali Khan became the Seventh Nizam, he suspected that Kishen Pershad was one of those nobles who had petitioned to the viceroy against his accession. He therefore, dismissed him. Kishen Pershad's alleged signatures on the petition later proved to be a forgery but Pershad had to wait for sixteen years to rehabilitate himself.

He then travelled in India extensively. He learnt painting adding one more to his varied hobbies including playing on the harmonium and sitar, and cooking. On a visit to Lahore, he developed a deep and abiding friendship with the famous poet Dr Mohammad Iqbal. He himself wrote poetry in Persian and Urdu and sported the pen name of '*Shad*' (The Happy One). His palace became renowned for its *mushairas* (Urdu poetic gatherings) where the best poets of India recited their compositions. His were the only *mushairas* at which the Nizam's poems could be recited. Kishen Pershad used to receive the poems by touching them to his forehead and eyes and then give them to the messenger for recitation. Every line in it was so vociferously lauded as if the poet himself was present. One of the poets in his *mushairas* used to be Abid Ali sporting the feminine pen-name 'Begum'. He dressed, wrote and recited as if he was a woman. He thus provided a humorous touch to the proceedings. In one *mushaira,* he read a couplet in which he expressed gratitude to his patron Maharaja Kishen Pershad who had granted him a monthly stipend. Using a double entendre, he said, 'Thanks to the Maharaja, I still get my monthly.' The Maharaja retorted, 'Strange, I have grown old but you still get your monthlies.'

Kishen Pershad also wrote prose, travelogues and authored over sixty books and pamphlets. Nawab Mehdi Nawaz Jung, who served as his secretary, believed that charity was his most outstanding virtue. According to Mohammed bin Ali Bawahb, his daily charities and alms giving amounted to ₹ 300. Whenever he travelled, he used to keep two bagfuls of coins in his car from which he threw handfuls with both hands to crowds of poor people who would chase his car. Once when he went to Ooty, the British government objected to his practice of throwing coins like that. Thereupon, he came back saying, 'How can I go out without doing that?'

He became prime minister again in 1927 and held that office for nine years.

Kishen Pershad was courteous and generous to a fault. He used to refer to himself as a *fakir* i.e. a person of no means. Given his lifestyle, his unbounded generosity, and the neglect of his estate, he ended up in debt.

Kishen Pershad was very secular in his outlook. He married three Hindu and four Muslim women and sired thirty children from them. Quite a few of them died during his lifetime. The children born of Muslim wives

Maharaja Kishen Pershad

were given Muslim names, brought up as Muslims, and married to Muslim spouses. Similarly, those born of Hindu wives followed their respective mothers' faith. This is perhaps the only example of a personage's children following the faith not of the father but of the mother. In his will, however, he advised the practice of monogamy.

Shad Nagar town in Mehboob Nagar district is named after his pen name.[40]

He enjoyed equal popularity amongst all the communities. Many people often said that he was a Muslim while others maintained that he was a Hindu. He responded with a couplet:

Mai hoon Hindu, main hoon Musalmaan, har mazhab hai mera imaan
'Shaad' ka mazhab 'Shaad' hee jaane Azaadi azaad hee jaane.
(I am a Hindu, I am a Muslim, and I belong to all religions
Only Shad knows his religion, just as only the Free know freedom)

He died in 1940 at the age of seventy-six. No trace was left of his palace, 'Shad Mansion', and other properties within about four decades of his demise.

HOW THE KING KOTHI GOT ITS NAME

The Seventh Nizam, Mir Osman Ali Khan, was born in the Purani Haveli in 1886 and stayed there through his early life. However, by that time the city had expanded a great deal; towards the north and east and after his accession in 1911, he wanted to move to the newer part of the city. When he was looking around for a suitable building he came upon one built by one of the Jamedars, Kamal Khan. The mansion was purchased from Kamal Khan and used as his residence. There was however, one hitch. Kamal Khan had put his initials 'KK' all over the building and even had it carved into its furniture and fittings. It was therefore a problem to remove those initials without disfiguring the building and furniture. Nawab Faridun-ul-Mulk suggested that instead of removing those initials, why not call the building 'King Kothi'? It was an appropriate name for the residence of the king, and obviated the need for removing the existing initials. It was a hybrid name half-English and half Urdu and sounds rather strange to Indian ears. However, this proposal was accepted by Mir Osman Ali Khan.[41]

The King Kothi complex had several buildings in two groups. The western half of the building was known as 'Nazri Bagh'. The Nizam used to stay there. The entrance to that had always a thick tarpaulin curtain

King Kothi Palace, Residence of the Seventh Nizam

draped on it. It therefore came to be known as the 'Purdah Gate'. In course of time, the purdah became quite shabby but it was not replaced. One could not imagine that the ruler of the largest Indian State and the richest man of the world had his residence behind that scruffy curtain.

Though he stayed in King Kothi, the Nizam visited the Purani Haveli regularly every evening to meet his mother. When he drove in the old car, the traffic on the route was stopped by the blow of four whistles of policemen on duty and people had to either to prostrate by way of respect to him, or to disappear into the adjoining streets.

The Nizam died in 1967. In 1980, the Government of Andhra Pradesh converted the eastern half of the building into a general hospital and named it the King Kothi Hospital. The Nazri Bagh area has been walled off and continues to belong to the private estate of the Nizam.

The Nazri Bagh is closed and is not open to the public. It is now in a dilapidated state and seems to be beyond repair due to its prolonged neglect.

NAZARS FOR THE NIZAMS

In 1739 when Nadir Shah invaded India and was marching towards Delhi, the Mughal Emperor summoned his governor of the Deccan, Mir Qamaruddin, the First Nizam of Hyderabad, to help him defend the country.

The Nizam accordingly proceeded to Delhi leaving his son Nasir Jung in charge of the Deccan province. Taking advantage of his father's absence, Nasir Jung raised the banner of rebellion. The Nizam rushed back to deal with his delinquent son. The battle between the father and son was joined near Daulatabad in 1741. Nasir Jung fought bravely but many nobles deserted him and he was easily routed. He was brought as a captive into the presence of his father.

After his victory, the Nizam's minister, Sayyad Lashkar Khan, offered a *nazar* to him for his success in crushing the rebellion. The Nizam accepted it as a token of the celebration of his victory.

Immediately thereafter, the minister offered another *nazar*.

'Why this second nazar, Khan?' asked the puzzled patriarch.

'Sire,' replied the minister respectfully, 'the first one was for your victory. The second is for the reason that your son has escaped injury on the battle-field and is safe.' The Nizam accepted it with a hint of a smile.

The Khan again got up and proffered a *nazar* for the third time.

A frown came over the Nizam's aging brow. 'What is this puzzle, my Khan? Why this third *nazar*?'

This time the minister too smiled and he made bold to explain. 'The name of the noble prince is Nasir Jung, my Lord. That means victory. The bearer of such a name should not retreat. And, God be praised, he has justified his name. It is God's grace and my Lord's sagacity that the affair has come to a proper conclusion. But the prince is not a coward.'

The Nizam beamed as he accepted the third *nazar*. How did the minister know that these were the exact thoughts going on in his mind too? When he had offered prayers to his Creator after crushing the rebellion, he too had thanked the Almighty for these very three things. A son is a son even in his rebellion. All fathers know that; however, very few sons realise that.

The father forgave the son. However, an example had to be made of him lest the Nizam should be taken as a soft ruler; Nasir Jung was kept under close watch for some time after the event.[42]

The practice of *nazar* as a tribute by subordinates to their superiors, as amends for any fault or as an extortionate levy is very old. It was widely followed by successive Nizams.

During the rule of the Fifth Nizam a British painter visited Hyderabad. The Nizam, the dewan and the painter visited the Golkonda fort. After a tiring visit, each one retired to their respective rooms to take rest. While the dewan had taken off his *dastar* – headdress, and loosened the *bugloos* – the waistband, suddenly the Nizam happened to look in for the minister for some consultation. Finding himself not appropriately dressed, the dewan got up and offered a *nazar* to the Nizam for his failure to be ever ready.

Maharaja Kishen Pershad narrates a famous incident in 1883 when the prime minister, Sir Salar Jung planned a tour of a part of the State for the young Nizam who was still under regency. He had taken along with him his two sons and Kishen Pershad for the adolescent Nizam's company. The Nizam's tutor, Captain Clerk, was also in the party.

When they reached Ahmedabad, a camp was ready so that the Nizam and his suite could freshen up, have their lunch, and get ready for the next leg of the journey.

Nazar Darbar of the Seventh Nizam

The Nizam liked the place so much that he told his companions that he would like to spend the day there and to proceed to Sholapur the next day.

Salar Jung did not like the idea and sent Captain Clerk to tell the Nizam that the programme had been notified in advance. Many dignitaries would be waiting for him and in the absence of a serious reason, it did not behove a ruler to change State programmes at whim. The Nizam was still adamant. When the tutor insisted, rather abruptly, the Nizam began to sob and said that the dewan and the tutor were making him run too much and imposing their will on him. He added defiantly, 'I will not go. Let us see what you can do to me!'

Captain Clerk came back and reported the Nizam's reaction.

After sometime, Mehboob came out of his tent and sent for the party. He sent word to the dewan to have lunch with him. Salar Jung came, salaamed the Nizam and offered a *nazar* to him apologising for his insolence.

Mehboob smiled, put both his hands on the dewan's bowed head, and said, 'You are right. One should be punctual and not change one's decisions unnecessarily.' Saying this, he gave him his diamond-studded gold watch as a gift.[43]

The custom of *nazar*-giving acquired a special importance during the rule of the Seventh Nizam. There were two official occasions for receiving *nazars* – the festival of Eid and the Nizam's birthday. All nobles, gazetted officers of the state, and anybody who mattered were required to offer a *nazar* to the Nizam. The minimum amount of the *nazar* was one gold coin and four silver pieces – ₹ 24. There was no maximum. A register was kept in which the names of the *nazar*-givers were noted.

If anyone wanted an audience with the Nizam, he had to present a *nazar* at the audience. There still are some septuagenarians who recall having presented a *nazar* to the Nizam as little children.

The Nizam had an extensive *jagir* of his own called *Sarf-e-khas*. Sometimes he would have a mango from his garden sent to someone's house. It was sent in style with about half-a-dozen liveried servants carrying the gift in a small procession. It was an honour noticed by the neighbours. The recipient had to acknowledge the honour by going to the King Kothi the next morning and present the prescribed *nazar*. There is a large canvas of the *nazar* darbar held to celebrate the silver jubilee of the Seventh Nizam in the foyer of the Jubilee Hall in the Public Garden.

Facing page: Falaknuma Palace, now a hotel with the Taj group, was presented to the Sixth Nizam as a nazar in 1897 by the Paigah noble, Sir Vicar-ul-Umra (prime minister 1894-1901). However, the Nizam paid for it enough to clear the former's debts *(courtesy Abhishek Patel)*

Sometimes the Nizam would send a part of the *khasa* – the royal dinner – to a chosen person. He had to acknowledge the honour by paying the *nazar* the next morning.

It was a good way to make money. Part of the reason for his acquiring the reputation of the richest man in the world was his fine art of adding *nazars* to his private kitty.

The practice was severely criticised by the Resident and in a letter dated 17 March 1923, he advised the Nizam to stop it. In the second Hyderabad Political Conference at Mumbai in 1926, Y.M. Kale attacked the system. The Nizam first defended it and then issued orders restricting it.

In 1945, the young Raja Rameshwar Rao of the Wanaparthy *samasthan* received a packet of eight mangoes from the Nizam with a note scribbled by the Nizam: 'For this no *nazar* need be presented'.[44]

USTAD TO TWO NIZAMS

Hafiz Jaleel Hassan 'Jaleel' Manikpuri came to Hyderabad in 1900, and like Dagh had to wait for a long time before fortune smiled on him.

In 1905, the prime minister, Maharaja Kishen Pershad, organised a *mushaira* on the silver jubilee of the Nizam. The Nizam, Mir Mehboob Ali Khan himself attended it. All the leading poets were also there.

Since it was a special jubilee *mushaira*, only *qasidas* (odes of praise) in honour of the Nizam, were to be recited. The length of each poem was restricted to twelve couplets. A tall candle in a gold stand with the personal emblem of Kishen Pershad was kept in the centre. Overhead hung a giant chandelier.

The walls of the hall had life-size mirrors in gilded frames. The host said a few words of welcome to his ruler, congratulated him on his silver jubilee and wished him many more. After that, the master of ceremonies gave a brief introduction of all the poets. As each poet was introduced, he got up and made seven salaams to the royal guest. Then, the proceedings began.

Normally, a *mushaira* is a loud affair and there is no dearth of praise even from rival poets by way of professional courtesy. Somehow, this sitting was going flat. There was no applause, no calls for *encore*. After a while the Nizam who sat impassively reclining against a bolster, whispered something to the host. Kishen Pershad, in an attempt to enliven the proceedings, broke the order of roll call and invited the newcomer Jaleel to recite his poem. He was an instant success. The Nizam who was almost dozing off with boredom sat up and exclaimed in praise '*Wah, Wah!*' '*Marhaba.*' Everyone else followed him vociferously.

Jaleel could not cope with the shouts of praise and he had to stop mid-way at every line to acknowledge the cheers by salaaming, and in response to shouts for *encore*, had to repeat his lines - some, many times. When the sitting was over at 4 a.m. and the poets started leaving, Jaleel was asked to stay back. The Nizam wanted to hear his poem again. He had liked it very much.

Jaleel Manikpuri

After about a year, at a ceremony in his palace for the start of teaching of the holy Quran to a prince, Mehboob had composed a poem but was not satisfied with it. He was stuck on some word. He asked Jaleel for help. Many drafts were made. Only the fourth attempt satisfied him.

A few days later Jaleel was appointed royal tutor on five hundred rupees a month. He was also appointed a courtier and given the title of 'Fasahat Jung'.

When Mehboob died in 1911 and Mir Osman Ali Khan succeeded him,

Jaleel's appointment was renewed making him the new ruler's tutor and companion.

Jaleel was required to attend the court daily and had to compose at least one poem every day and sometimes more on different occasions of all sorts. The Nizam used to send his compositions to Jaleel's house through a special messenger in a sealed cover. They had to be returned corrected the same day. The bearer would wait on until they were corrected. Some days a dozen poems would come one after the other. The *ustad* had to be available from around 8 a.m. to 10 p.m. because the special courier could come any time.

The Nizam used to write with a pencil on both sides of scraps of paper. Sometimes he wrote on the flap of a cigarette packet if that was the only thing handy at that time. Apart from the needed corrections, which had to be made in very respectful terms, the *ustad*'s opinion had also to be given on each couplet and all possible praise showered on those, which needed no amendment. Remarks like 'Excellent, Congratulations.' 'Superb. What an idea!' 'One in a million; My humble praise,' etc, were made in the margin or below a given word or phrase. In addition, a general assessment had to be given on the poem as a whole and it had better be positive. While the poem was written in pencil, the amendments were made in red ink. They were published in the front page of local Urdu papers along with the corrections.

The *ustad* could not give tuition to anybody else except Kishen Pershad.

In the royal sittings, only the Nizam's poetry was recited and the *ustad* was expected to make instant corrections. Jaleel had also to help the Nizam compose chronograms in verse wherever the occasion demanded. Sometimes the Nizam would give just a line and the *ustad* had to compose one or more poems based on the meter and rhyme of the given line.

The job of the *ustad* was therefore not easy and required, perhaps, more than proficiency in prosody, an astuteness to survive. However, Jaleel did well and served successfully two Nizams from 1909 until his death in 1946. In due course, his salary was increased from five hundred to one thousand rupees a month. By a strange accounting procedure, the salary was paid from the State exchequer but routed through the personal estate office of the Nizam – *Sarf-e-khas* (crown lands). Once, as a measure of economy, the salaries of all *Sarf-e-khas* employees were reduced by half. Jaleel too suffered the cut. Then, some auditor pointed out that the cut would not apply to Jaleel because he was being paid by the State. The *Sarf-e-khas* was only a disbursing agency and all the while, it was receiving the full amount from the State exchequer. The cut was restored but the arrears were not paid to him. The Nizam told Jaleel not to worry; his arrears – of about one lakh rupees – were intact; they were with the Nizam as his trust, and would be paid to Jaleel whenever he needed them. Jaleel never got the amount!

His son, Ali Ahmed Jaleeli was also a good poet. He did a PhD thesis on his father.[45]

THE SEVENTH NIZAM AS POET & PUBLISHER

Four out of the seven Nizams of Hyderabad were poets. The first two wrote in Persian and the last two both in Persian as well as in Urdu. The last two had also employed poetic preceptors.

The *ustad* had to be available at all times of the day and night. There was no knowing when the Nizam would get inspiration to compose a couplet or a *ghazal*. As soon as that happened, it was rushed to the teacher for necessary action. Sometimes only an idea would strike him and the *ustad* had to give it shape and form. It was a most delicate job and needed a lot of tact. The corrections and improvements in the ruler's composition were made in a most respectful

The Seventh Nizam writing a poem

manner. If the *ustad* had to modify a word or a phrase, he first praised the original in superlatives, congratulated the royal pupil and then suggested that in his 'humble opinion' it could perhaps be put differently!

The last Nizam used often to send his poems to local newspapers. They had to be published on the front page prominently along with the modifications suggested by the *ustad*. By the time he was about thirty, the ruler had composed a large number of poems in different genres and so decided to publish an anthology. In that connection, he issued a detailed *firman*, a royal order, on 18 February 1919. It is amusing to note some of the contents of that order:

- 'My *ghazals* which represent my random thoughts and which number 750 have been published in six separate volumes containing 125 ghazals each. All interested readers and critics are informed that they can obtain them at one guinea per copy. The second edition will not be published unless it becomes necessary.
- Every purchaser will have to buy all the six sets. Single volumes will not be sold.
- The price i.e. six guineas will be uniform for all buyers within the State and outside.
- The purchaser will bear the postal expenses.
- Every volume will carry an official seal. In the absence of that, it will be deemed to have been stolen.
- Printing any copy of these volumes is forbidden. Anyone found doing so would be responsible for the consequences.
- The books will be sold within a month and can be had from Nazri Bagh (Nizam's palace).
- The price is to be paid in advance.

- A copy of the above order should be published in the Gazette Extraordinary.

A guinea was one pound and one shilling and at that time was equal to ₹ 21. In those days, a book of that size in Urdu would ordinarily sell for a fraction of a rupee.

Needless to say that the sets sold out in no time. All those who wished to demonstrate their loyalty to the young ruler purchased copies at that exorbitant price.

It is a pity that none of those volumes is available today.

Once, some claque amongst the courtiers praised the Nizam's poetry to the skies and suggested that it deserved to be prescribed as a text for the graduate course in the Osmania University. The Nizam approved the idea. Moulvi Abdul Haq, popularly known as the 'Father of Urdu' was the professor of Urdu at the University and it fell to his lot to implement the orders. He was in a fix. If he did not carry out the edict, he would attract the royal ire; on the other hand, if he obeyed, he would become the laughing stock amongst men of letters. He sought an audience to attempt to get the orders cancelled. When he reached the Presence, he saw the Nizam sitting in his usual old easy chair. Manzoor Jung, Hosh Bilgrami, and Zain Yar Jung were standing in front of him.

'Yes, Moulvi. Have you seen our orders?' asked the Nizam as he saw the savant.

'Yes, *Ala Hazrat*,' submitted the professor as he made the customary seven bows, 'I am here in that connection. Your compositions are royal amongst verses. What can be a greater honour for me than to explicate them to our students? However, my humble submission is that this worthless creature lacks the necessary depth of scholarship to be able to explain it adequately

Moulvi Abdul Haq

to students. Your Lordship's slave thought of presenting himself before His Master many times in order to obtain adequate understanding of the subtle points in the royal verses but I couldn't gather enough courage for fear that if in spite of the expostulation of His Exalted Highness, my limited brains could not grasp them, then what would I do?'

The Nizam looked at his acolyte, Hosh Bilgrami and chuckled: 'Do you hear what he says?' Hosh stepped forward with folded hands. 'Yes, *Ala Hazrat*, the royal composition is indeed royal amongst the common compositions. It is not easy to explain it.'

'You are right,' observed the Nizam, 'If the teacher himself can't understand, what will he explain to the students? That is right. But,' he added after a pause, 'how long do you think it will take for the University to get such teachers who can appreciate my poetry adequately?'

'Exalted Highness,' submitted Hosh, 'it depends not on the poetry but on the intelligence of the reader.'

'Right you are. It is intelligence that matters. I can give them my poems, but I can't invest in them the intelligence necessary to grasp them. Cancel the orders for teaching my poems in the University. Let the teachers understand them first.'

So, the 'mad' Moulvi, as the Nizam used to call Professor Abdul Haq, saved the students from the imposition – and his own face amongst the academia.[46]

Some of the Nizam's poems were translated into English by Sir Nizamat Jung, a Cantabrian and a former judge and minister of Hyderabad who himself was a very good poet in English. Some of them were reproduced in D.F. Karaka's biographical book on the Nizam: *The Fabulous Mogul*.

Such was the urge of the Nizam for writing poetry, that after India became a republic on 26 January 1950, and he became the Raj Pramukh of Hyderabad, he composed a poem in Persian to mark the event. He had it translated into English by Sir Nizamat and sent the original along with its English translation to the chief minister of Hyderabad, M.K. Vellodi, addressing him as 'My dear Friend'. In his covering letter marked 'Personal', he wrote: 'I shall be grateful if you kindly forward this to the high authorities in Delhi, on my behalf, and ask them that if they have no objection, I would like this poem to published in English papers in India, in commemoration of that historic declaration as it was a unique event in the annals of India'. He signed it as 'Nizam VII (MOAK)'. The initials stood for Mir Osman Ali Khan.

The chief minister wrote to V.P. Menon who was secretary of the ministry of states of India. Menon showed the letter to prime minister Nehru. He felt that it would be better if both the original and the translation were published together. When this view was conveyed to the Nizam, he sent both the versions with a letter to say that the translation could never convey the original sense fully. The 16-line poem concluded:

The New Dawn's greetings, 'OSMAN,' rich and strange,
And the four quarters hail the promised change!

However, it is not known whether any paper published the poem.

The number of his poems was indeed very large. He had established a trust and appointed a committee for publishing his poems in Persian and Urdu. The Trustees thought it would take a long time to sift through the whole body of his outpourings and so decided to publish two volumes in the first instance. Accordingly, in 1975, the Trust published one volume of three hundred poems in Urdu and Persian covering four different genres.[47]

A PROPHET FOR INDIA

Ghulam Akbar Khan, a Pathan from UP came to Hyderabad in 1893. After taking his law degree, he became a junior to his cousin, Fida Husain Khan, the father of Zakir Husain who rose to be President of India (1967-69). In 1918, he was appointed a judge of the newly constituted High Court of Hyderabad with the title of Nawab Akbar Yar Jung.

On 11 August 1936, the Young Men's Kayasth Union organised a function on Janamashtami (the birthday of Lord Krishna). It was held in the mansion of Raja Narsing Raj Bahadur 'Aali' at Hussaini Alam and was presided over by Mirza Yar Jung Bahadur, chief justice of the State. Akbar Yar Jung delivered the keynote address entitled 'Shri Krishna: The Prophet of Hind'. In his brilliant address in Urdu, laced with quotations from Arabic and Persian, he made the bold assertion that Lord Krishna was indeed a prophet like others mentioned in the Quran, the holy book of Islam.

The thrust of his lucid speech, and his interpretations and deductions were based mainly on the Islamic exegesis, namely, the verses of the Quran, the sayings of the Prophet and commentaries of some of the enlightened and liberal scholars of the faith. His main proposition was based on two verses of the Quran. *Ayat* 7 of *Sura* 13 declares 'and for every people there has been a guide'. Later, in *Ayat* 40 of *Sura* 78 it is stated that 'certainly we sent apostles before thee; there are some of them that we have mentioned to thee and others whom we have not mentioned.'

From this major premise of the Quran, Akbar Yar Jung postulated that 'if therefore Shri Krishna is not mentioned by name in the Quran, it was no reason to doubt his prophethood. Would you believe that a nation whose civilisation and culture had spread over such a large part of Asia, whose philosophy and learning had influenced Greece and Egypt, was left without a guide and teacher?' Then he affirmed: 'These teachers are styled variously by some as *rishis* and *munis* and by others as *nabis* and *paighambars*, etc. Amongst these there was one holy personage, whose birth we are here to celebrate. I mean Shri Krishna, whom in my religious phraseology I would call Krishna *alai, his salam* ('upon whom be peace!'). I have no hesitation in regarding this great personage, whom the Hindus consider an avatar of God, as a *nabi* ('a prophet of God'). I therefore offer him the salutations due to the prophets.'

Nawab Akbar Yar Jung

Then he went on to underline the doctrine that according to the teaching of the Quran, a Muslim can make no distinction between the prophets. 'Even as they regard Noah, Abraham, Moses and Jesus (upon all of whom be peace!) as prophets of God, so do they regard the prophets of all nations.'[48]

Akbar Yar Jung used a benediction for Krishna - 'may peace be upon him' - which the Muslims use only for their acknowledged prophets. This act aroused the ire of a section of the orthodox theologians. One, Aini Shah Nizami, wrote in the *Subeh Deccan*, an Urdu daily, in its issue of 19 August, 1936, accusing the speaker of 'innovative flight of imagination' which went beyond the pale of conventional and traditional Muslim beliefs and which, according to him, might not even be acceptable to the orthodox Hindus. On his promptings, the Seventh Nizam, Mir Osman Ali Khan, also wrote his personal comments in the same paper on 22 August, 1936 adding an admonition that government 'officials should refrain from making public speeches on controversial themes, religious or political, that might upset prevailing peace and harmony.' He also warned editors of newspapers against printing such controversial speeches or articles.

It was rumoured that at that time the Nizam was being pressurised to banish Akbar Yar Jung from the State for his heretical utterances. However, he did not do so probably because both he and the prime minister, Maharaja Kishen Pershad, held him in high regard and were not inclined to take any extreme step to penalise him. Indeed, such was his reputation that within four months of that speech, when he reached the age of superannuation, he was given an extraordinary extension of two years as judge of the High Court, and was nominated as a member of the Legislative Council, which he served from 1936 to 1940.

In the gathering communal gloom of 1936, it was indeed an act of extraordinary courage on the part of a Muslim official to come out with such an interpretation. He risked a great deal by that. It was sheer good luck that he did not come to harm.

THE ROMANCE OF BELLA VISTA

The Seventh Nizam had a number of wives and concubines and sired many children. Only two of his sons from his principal wife, Dulhan Pasha, enjoyed official recognition. The elder, Mir Himayat Ali Khan was formally known as Azam Jah. He was born in February 1907. In 1936, under an agreement with the British, he was given the title of Prince of Berar through ironically Berar had ceased to be a part of Hyderabad in 1853.

His younger brother, Mir Shuja'at Ali Khan formally known as Muazzam Jah was born nine months after his elder brother, in November 1907. He was called the Junior Prince and was the chairman of the City Improvement Board. He was a poet sporting the pen name of *'Shajih'* (meaning 'the brave one'). He stayed in the Hill Fort Palace at the foot of *Naubat Pahad* commanding a grand view of the Hussain Sagar Lake.

Born in the same year, the two brothers were married on the same day on 12 November 1931 at Nice in France. Azam Jah, the Prince of Berar, was married to the daughter and the only child of Abdul Majid, the last caliph of Islam and sultan of Turkey who had been deposed in 1924. His bride,

Facing page: Hussain Sagar Lake just after sunset

Princess Durru Shehvar (literally, the great pearl) was a tall, stately and beautiful young lady of about eighteen. The Junior Prince was married to a first cousin of Durru Shehvar called Niloufer (meaning lotus). She was about two years younger than her cousin.

The Nizam did not go for the wedding. Nor did any member of the immediate family. Only some members of the ex-sultan's family at Nice, some Turkish nobles and a few friends attended the wedding on behalf of the brides. The grooms were accompanied by an official delegation led by Sir Akbar Hydari. The ex-caliph himself conducted the religious ceremony. A holiday was declared in Hyderabad in celebration of the wedding.

The princes with their brides returned to Hyderabad on 31 December 1931. The city was illuminated and the local newspapers brought out special illustrated editions to mark the occasion.

The official residence of the Prince of Berar was called 'Bella Vista'. It was constructed in 1905 by Muslehuddin Mohammed, Hakim-ud-dowla, chief justice of the High Court of Hyderabad at a cost of ₹ 45,000.

After his death, the Nizam bought the mansion for ₹ 60,000 in 1917.

During Azam Jah's occupation of the mansion lasting more than two decades, night was day and

Prince of Berar with wife Durru Shehvar and son Mukarram Jah
Facing page: Durru Shehvar

day was night. Revelries lasted throughout the night and, as the dawn broke, the prince and his protégés retired to their beds.

Durru Shehvar and her cousin Niloufer were reckoned as two of the most beautiful women of their times. Their marriages did not work and Durru Shehvar moved to England where she stayed till her death in 2000, visiting Hyderabad once a year or so.

The two princes were paid a net monthly allowance of ₹ 25, 000 each. But they lived such a lavish life that they could not manage within that amount. They incurred huge debts from all and sundry. The creditors preserved the credit notes carefully and at one time the Nizam cleared the debts of the two princes, which reportedly amounted to about ₹ 4.5 crores. Simultaneously, he issued a *firman* warning the princes and all creditors that he would not be responsible for any further liabilities of the princes.

Princess Durru Shehvar loved outdoor life. She played tennis and liked to swim and ride. The princess also patronised local social clubs and charities. When she came to live at Bella Vista, she had a large swimming pool built there. She tried to persuade her husband to learn swimming. Jeelani, a young champion swimmer was summoned for that purpose.

'You are a champion swimmer, I understand,' the prince asked Jeelani.

'I am a humble swimmer, Your Highness,' replied the athletic young man.

'I bet you can't teach me swimming,' the Prince declared dismissively.

'I shall try my best, Sir. And there is no reason why *Sirkar* should not excel in it.'

'I am telling you, you just cannot teach me swimming. I bet.'

Then the prince elaborated: 'How can you teach me swimming when I won't even enter the pool?' Saying that, the Prince broke into a guffaw at his own wisecrack. Jeelani was relieved. A small baby-size pool was built in which the Prince could wallow like a child while the Princess dived and swam in her big pool.[49]

The two Turkish princesses soon discovered the incompatibility between them and their husbands. It was a union of two contrasting cultures – the Western and the Mughalai – and hence doomed to failure.

The Bella Vista swarmed with women of all types. The Nizam became so disgusted with them that on 23 January 1956 he issued the following *firman*:

> 'Appendix to the Text of the Refreshing Tidings' (published last Friday in the *Shiraz*')
>
> HEH was pleased to state that now the Committee to investigate the indebtedness of Bella Vista would start its work soon under my directions.
>
> However, the question of the ladies of Bella Vista is separate. Therefore, everything in that connection, that is, their status,

Bella Vista front view

Bella Vista Illuminated *(Courtesy Abhishek Patel)*

their family and on what conditions they were brought there and whether they have any written proof in favour of their claims – all these issues will have to be submitted before the Committee by the relatives of these ladies so that every case is scrutinised and decided on its merit. In the absence of these, they will be told that since they did all this on their own volition, Nazri Bagh (Nizam's Mansion in the King Kothi) has no responsibility for them. It should therefore be appropriate that they should be grateful for whatever treatment they have so far received from the Senior Prince (which is more than what their status called for) and go back to their houses. Their welfare lies in that. Clothes and jewellery worth thousands that have been given to them will not be taken back from them. Treating this as a favour, it will be

in their interest that they depart from Bella Vista. Otherwise they will harm themselves. If however, there are any special cases, as has been mentioned above, they will be separately considered because not all five fingers of hand are equal. So whatever decision is taken, it will be in the light of that and will be in accordance with some principles and rules so that it is considered just and the present complications are removed and the rest of the life of the resident of Bella Vista can be spent in peace and comfort. The head of the family considers a part of his responsibility to do such a thing.

The Prince of Berar was impatient to succeed to the *gaddi* of Hyderabad. He felt frustrated that whereas his father had become Nizam at the age of twenty-five, he was going on fifty and still waiting. He therefore organised black magic and secret prayers and *mannats* seeking the early demise of his father. One Moulana Abdul Qadeer Badayuni was sent every year for special prayers to Baghdad. His own ADC went to all the holy Muslim places in India with the same objective.[50]

The news reached the Nizam and he was greatly upset. In 1964, the Nizam fell seriously ill. The prince wrote to the Government of India asking them to declare him the Nizam. This was too much for the Nizam to bear. He decided to supercede him as his successor, nominating instead his grandson, Prince Mukarram Jah. This naturally created hostility between the father and the son and they never spoke to each other.

On the integration of the state with India in 1948, the mansion was converted into a State Guest House. I have stayed in the luxurious guesthouse at a very nominal tariff. The bearers were all liveried and the crockery and cutlery carried the official insignia of *Amira* in Urdu (meaning Royal). We moved around in the old state cars with separate seating for ADCs. The staff had very juicy stories to tell the guests.

In 1957, the Administrative Staff College of India was set up in the building, which was purchased from the state government. It became a premier training institution for senior civil servants and corporate executives on the lines of the British Staff College at Henley-on-Thames.

Amongst the recreational facilities for the participants, there was also a bar and the joke was that the college was attached to a bar. The bar was closed on the eve of the visit of the then prime minister, Morarji Desai on 3 January 1979.

THE HILL FORT PALACE

While the elder son of the Seventh Nizam stayed in the Bella Vista, the younger one was lodged in the Hill Fort Palace which also afforded a grand view of the Hussain Sagar Lake from a different angle.

It was built by Sir Nizamat Jung, a cousin of the builder of the Bella Vista. He too rose to be chief justice and later a minister of the Hyderabad State. In 1913, he suffered an attack of asthma. The doctors advised him to stay in an open place with fresh air. Accordingly, he bought five acres of land overlooking the Husain Sagar Lake for ₹ 100 to build his new residence.

The architectural style of the building was based on the style of the Trinity College in Cambridge where Nizamat Jung had studied, and the castles described in the novels of Sir Walter Scott. He completed the construction in 1915 and named it 'Hill Fort'. He lived in it for fifteen years. After his retirement in 1929, he went on a pilgrimage to Mecca. On return, he decided to live a simpler life and so decided to sell the property. He had spent ₹ 100,000 on the construction. He had taken two loans from the government - one for the construction of the building, and the other for purchasing a car. After adjusting the arrears of the two loans, he fixed the

Hill Fort Palace

sale price of the property at ₹ 67,000. He refused to take any appreciation on the value for the property.

The Nizam bought it and allotted it to the Junior Prince, Muazzam Jah as his official residence in his capacity as the chairman of the City Improvement Board. It thus became a palace.

The prince was a poet and used to live lavishly, and held his 'court' at about 7 p.m. Every evening he invited a selected gathering of nobles and some poets to dine with him. After dinner, a *mehfil* was arranged which lasted throughout the night. In that *mehfil* professional singers used to sing his poems and often *mujras* were also held. The 'court' was dismissed at about five in the morning after which the prince would take two sleeping pills and go to bed. Some well-known poets of Urdu in the country came to be associated with his 'court'. The prince used to compose lyrical poetry of a lighter type. They are occasionally heard in some parties even now.

On every Eid, he used to buy a new set of *sherwani* and *pajama* for all his courtiers. For his own, he used to go to 'Burton's Shop' in Secunderabad. During his visit, the shop was closed to all other customers except the wives of European military officers. The prince never purchased a piece; he bought a whole roll. The point was that nobody else should have a *sherwani* made of a cloth similar to his.

He used to send his agents to different parts of the country to select and invite singers and dancers for the Eid festival. Valuable gifts were given to them on their departure. Amongst them was the renowned ghazal singer Begum Akhtar who at that time was known as Akhtari Bai Faizabadi. There is an interesting account of her visit and other goings-on in the palace by a regular poet - courtier, Sidq Jaisi. I have translated his book in Urdu to English with introduction and notes.[51] One evening while the dinner was on in the

Prince Muazzam Jah, Junior Prince

Princesses Durru Shehvar and Niloufer

lawns of the palace it started raining but nobody got up because the prince kept sitting there.

After seventeen years of unhappy marriage, princess Niloufer went away to France in 1948 and asked for a divorce. She later married an American ex-army man and film director named Pope. In spite of fervent pleas by both her husband and the Nizam, Niloufer did not relent. The stunning beauty that she was, Niloufer became a part of the high society scene in Paris. She nursed an ambition of becoming a film star and there was no problem in that. Somehow, it never came to pass.

From France, she sent a donation for the establishment of a hospital for children and women. Completed in 1955, the Niloufer Hospital for Women and Children is adorned with her portrait in its foyer.

The Seventh Nizam died at 1:22 in the afternoon of 26 February 1967. As usual, Muazzam Jah was fast asleep at that time. When his ADC tried to wake him up, he snubbed him saying, 'Don't bring such bad news so early in the morning'! He did not attend his father's funeral.

After the integration of Hyderabad with India, the Hill Fort Palace became the property of the government. It became the office of the Development Commissioner of the government of Hyderabad. The prince moved out to stay in the 'Fern Villa' – the former residence of the former superintendent of Public Gardens and the legendary wit of Hyderabad, Jamaluddin.

Princess Niloufer

The prince expired in 1987. Niloufer died in France in 1989 aged seventy-three.

In 1955, the Hill Fort Palace was leased to the Ritz Hotel. For many years, it was the most modern and the best hotel in Hyderabad. It retained its old world charm till the very end and many old-timers used to prefer to stay there rather than the more modern hotel which came up later in the city.

In 1989, the government terminated the lease and after protracted legal battle, ultimately the building reverted to the government in 1997. There were various proposals as to its best use - as a government guest house or residence for the chief minister, or as a heritage hotel. However, as of date, it lies unused.

THE WIT-LAUREATE OF HYDERABAD

Jamaluddin was a great wit who made many jokes. His name also generated many jokes even after his death.

He was born in 1881 in Chennai into a family related to Tippu Sultan. He came to Hyderabad as a student, and studied up to matriculation.

Jamaluddin married Ghousia Begum, sister of Nawab Kazim Yar Jung who was a favourite of the Seventh Nizam (1911-1948). He was the Nizam's minister-in-waiting for many years. Ghousia Begum was one of the first women graduates of the Hyderabad State. She was sent for training to England in the Montessori system of education for children. On return, she introduced the system in the State.

Due to his relationship with Nawab Kazim Yar Jung, Jamaluddin also came close to the Nizam. He was appointed superintendent of the Public Gardens.

After training in gardening in Japan, Jamaluddin prepared a project for setting up a Chinese Section in the Public Garden. He promised the Nizam that it would cost one-lakh rupees and take a year to complete. Unexpectedly, the Nizam came to inspect the progress exactly after a year. The garden was far from ready and so Jamaluddin hurriedly put some

Jamaluddin, the wit-laureate of Hyderabad with his wife

potted plants to give it the semblance of a garden. When the Nizam pulled him up for not sticking to his commitment, Jamaluddin replied, 'Your Exalted Highness, it is all ready except for one thing. Only volcanoes have to be imported from Japan!' The Nizam smiled and went away. Nobody else could ever fob off the Nizam like that.

Later, the Chinese Section became the best part of the Public Garden. Jamaluddin's sense of humour brought him close to many high personages including the Prince of Berar and the Junior Prince. The princes had their own set of courtiers and nobody could be a member of both. Jamaluddin was the only exception. He dined with the latter and the former often dropped in at the Public Gardens during his riding to have a chat or even a cup of tea with him.

Jamaluddin built a house for himself in the Red Hills in 1940 and called it the 'Fern Villa'. It had a hall built and decorated in the Japanese style.

Because of his unrestrained wit, many jokes came to be attributed to him - some real and some apocryphal.

A favourite was that Jamaluddin used to wear his headdress with the front facing backwards. When someone asked him why, he replied, 'What if the Nizam suddenly comes from behind?'

Once the driver of his car asked for a screwdriver. He said, 'What is the need of a screwdriver when there is already a driver?'

Once his servant was trying to fix a nail on the wall. Jamaluddin noticed that the head of the nail was towards the wall while the pointed end was facing the hammer. He pulled up the servant and said, 'The nail in your hand is the wrong one. It is meant for the opposite wall!'

One day, his driver suddenly applied brakes to the car. 'Why?' he asked the driver. The driver said that there was a pit on the road. 'Then why didn't you blow the horn?' asked Jamaluddin angrily.

K.P.S. Menon, the well-known Indian diplomat, in his autobiography *Many Worlds Revisited* narrates the incident of Jamaluddin's opposition to the suggestion of sending his daughter for higher education to Delhi. He said that it was not safe to send young girls to such far-away places alone. 'She might get involved with somebody there.' However, he was prevailed upon to let her go. After some time his daughter wrote to him saying how much she liked the college and that she had picked up a number of friends. She added that she had become very fond of Ping-Pong. On reading this letter, Jamaluddin flared up, 'I warned you. See, now she has got involved with a Chinese fellow.'

When he died in 1942, the Nizam himself composed his chronogrammatic epitaph, which, besides paying him a tribute, also yielded the date of his death.

When N.T. Rama Rao became chief minister in 1983, he turned the Chinese Garden into an open-air theatre. Part of it was given to the Telugu University which he set up.

Over the years, as often happens, so many jokes were pasted on to him and he became known more for his wit than for his profession.[52]

CHUNNU NAWAB & THE 'BALISHTER'

In 1919, after a spell of ruling without a prime minster, Nizam VII set up an executive council with a president instead of a prime minister, Sir Ali Imam was a prominent barrister of Bihar. He had served as a member of the executive council of the viceroy and he was a member of the executive council of Bihar and Orissa. He was selected for the job.

A year before his appointment, as a barrister, Sir Ali Imam had occasion to visit Hyderabad in connection with a court case. When his train stopped at Veyjapur station, he saw a huge fawning crowd gathered around a bulky, pompous fellow at the platform. While people were paying their respects to him, liveried peons were rushing in and out of the train loading the first-class compartment with suitcases, trunks, bedrolls, tiffin-carriers, fruit baskets, bouquets, spittoons, silver tumblers, towels, a small carpet for prayers, and numerous other oddments.

When the train started, the beefy official looked at Sir Ali Imam condescendingly and introduced himself. 'I am Zain-ul-Abideen, tahsildar of the taluk. I am popularly known as Chunnu Nawab. I am going to Hyderabad on leave'. He then asked Sir Ali his name. 'Ali Imam' He had never heard of the name before and concluded that obviously he was a man of no consequence. 'What do you do for a living?' he asked. Sir Ali, not too keen to engage in a conversation, replied matter-of-factly that he was a barrister.

'What is a balishter?'

'It is a sort of advocate, a *vakil*.'

'Oh, *vakil*! Many *vakil*s appear in my court. Have you ever appeared in the court of a tahsildar?'

On receiving a negative reply, he invited Sir Ali Imam to witness the glory of his court and to appear there someday. While jabbering away without a pause, he was chewing pan and using the spittoon.

Chunnu Nawab then asked Ali Imam how much he earned. Sir Ali Imam replied modestly that he earned well enough to provide for his *daal* and *roti*. Chunnu Nawab remarked condescendingly that *daal* and *roti* were for the poor. He should have higher aspirations – for chicken and fish, which are the proper meal for the well-to-do. He then proceeded to advise him to give up barristership and take up the job of tahsildar. He boasted that though his salary was only ₹ 200 a month, it was just his pocket money. He earned a lot 'from above'. 'A tahsildar is the uncrowned king of the taluk, you know. He had to have the knack for making money.'

At the next station, a bearer of the Brandon Catering Company came to take orders for lunch. Sir Ali Imam was about to order when the tahsildar prevented him from doing so and said that he had enough to feed a whole compartment and he would take it as an insult

Sir Ali Imam

if the *balishter saab* did not break bread with him. However, he asked the bearer to bring half-a-dozen lemonades and sodas. Ali Imam asked him why he was ordering so many sodas and lemonades for just the two of them. Chunnu Nawab said that it was a matter of status. A tahsildar could not order just one or two sodas. Whatever was left would be consumed by the servants. At every station where the train stopped, some people came and made their offerings to the worthy official. It was very amusing and educative for Sir Ali Imam to see the fuss which people made about the tahsildar and how tahsildars battened themselves on the people.

Some months later Sir Ali Imam came to Hyderabad as president of the Nizam's Executive Council (prime minister). The memory of his earlier encounter with the great tahsildar was etched in his mind and so he sent for 'the uncrowned king of the taluk'. Chunnu Nawab came dressed formally in *sherwani* and *bugloos*. He made four nervous floor-salaams and stood erect like a statue before the premier, his eyes riveted on the carpet.

Sir Ali tried to put him at ease by asking him how he was doing. The tahsildar replied very humbly that by the grace of Almighty and the kindness of His Excellency he was doing well. Imam then referred to their meeting the previous year in the train. The tahsildar feigned surprise and promptly denied that he had ever had the honour of meeting the dignitary before. All the forensic skill of the barrister came to naught before the astute flunkey. He said; 'Your Honour, it must be a mix-up. However, it is my good luck to have the unique honour to have met the prime minister. I will never forget this rare privilege and will recount my great luck to my progeny.'

He then asked obsequiously if there were any orders for that speck of dust, that is, he. Ali Imam understood the reason for the 'king of the taluk' not wanting to be identified. After all, he was the tahsildar of the old school and had acquired a 'knack' of which he had boasted in the train. He had dealt with many rogues and to dispose of a mere prime minister was no big deal for him. Ali Imam gave up in despair and wished him well.

Zain-ul-Abideen, alias Chunnu Nawab came out of the exalted office, wiped his perspiration, loosened his *bugloos* and *sherwani*, and scooted for his life. After some time and much thought, he decided to apply for premature retirement. It was prudent to forego a year of service than to risk confrontation with the prime minister. After all, it would not be easy even for the 'uncrowned king of a taluk' to bluff a prime minister and survive.[53]

WHEN THE NIZAM WEPT

In November, 1930, a public meeting was held in the Victory Playground to celebrate the birthday of Prophet Muhammad. A young man was moving his audience to tears by his oration. Midway through his speech, there was a general commotion. Policemen on duty started blowing whistles nervously. Mir Osman Ali Khan, the Seventh Nizam, had arrived unannounced to attend the meeting. The young speaker paused only for a while and then greeted the newcomer in an emotion-charged manner: 'O' crowned slave of Muhammad of Arabia, come, let me tell thee about the style of governance of that emperor of both the spiritual and the corporeal worlds.' Osman sat there completely mesmerised and like the hundreds amongst the audience, washed by the flood of words

Mir Osman Ali Khan the Seventh Nizam

coming from that young speaker, tears began to roll down his cheeks. He asked some of the telling sentences of the speech to be repeated, as people say 'encore' in *mushairas*.

About a week later, on 25 November, the orator received a *firman*. It read:

> 'The royal personage was delighted to hear your sermon and on the auspicious occasion of his birthday is pleased to confer the title of Bahadur Yar Jung on you.'

The young man was born in 1905 to a petty jagirdar of Lal Garhi. He was also a hereditary jamadar in the Irregular Forces of the Nizam.

Right from school days, he used to excel in declamation and became a popular orator. When Bahadur Khan inherited the *jagir* on the death of his father in 1923, he also inherited a debt of ₹ 4.5 lakhs. Within four years he set the affairs right and having cleared all the debts, doubled the income from his estate to ₹ 40, 000 per annum. In 1927, he started The Society for the Propagation of Islam. He was fond of reading, knew Urdu, Arabic, Persian, and English, and had a smattering knowledge of Telugu. Because of his oratorical skills, he became immensely popular and very close to the Muslim League leader, Jinnah, whose speeches he often interpreted from English into Urdu.

Bahadur Yar Jung

In 1938, he was elected president of the Majlis-e-Ittehad-ul-Musalmeen, (MIM or *Ittehad* for short) a society with a cultural and religious manifesto. However, it soon acquired political complexion and became aligned with the Muslim League in British India. He soon rose to be the supreme and unquestioned leader of the *Ittehad* and imparted a new militancy to it.

Bahadur Yar Jung noted the peculiar political situation of Hyderabad. It was a State with a Hindu population of eighty-seven per cent and a Muslim ruler. With the winds of change blowing all over and the talk of democracy and the demands for a responsible government, the control of power was bound to pass from the ruling Muslim minority to the Hindu majority. To perpetuate the existing state of affairs, heavily weighted in favour of Muslims, he propounded an ingenious theory. The Nizam claimed that, as a ruler, he was sovereign. In 1938, Bahadur Yar Jung enunciated the doctrine of *'Ana'l Malik'*, – 'We are the sovereign'. According to this theory, sovereignty did not vest in the ruler, but in the Muslim community. The Nizam was merely a symbol of that sovereignty. Every Muslim in the State thus became a participant and a sharer in sovereignty. It thus sought to make every Muslim a stakeholder in the campaign for protecting the sovereignty of Muslims and its symbol, the Nizam. It became the official doctrine of the *Ittehad* and Bahadur Yar Jung insisted that Hyderabad should be declared an Islamic State.

To make matters absolutely sure, the demographic balance of the State had to be altered. He therefore undertook a vigorous programme of conversion of Hindus to Muslims – particularly those belonging to the untouchable and backward classes in rural areas. His biography published in Pakistan, credits him with the conversion of 24,000 persons.

Bahadur Yar Jung thus reduced the Nizam from the personification of sovereignty to its mere symbol. He often said things, which caused the Nizam discomfiture, and not unoften, even offence. Once when he thundered against the British presence and their direction of administration in the State, the Nizam was compelled by the Resident to censure and to silence him and to order that he be confined to his house for some time. The jagirdars were not allowed to participate in politics. To overcome that constraint, Bahadur Yar Jung renounced his *jagir* and title in 1940 and intensified his activities. That added to his popularity.

In 1944, he had gone to a dinner at the house of Hashim Ali Khan, a judge of the High Court and a close friend. As soon as he sat down and took a pull at the hookah, he collapsed. Many people suspected that he was poisoned, possibly with the Nizam's connivance. However, the Nizam attended the funeral the next day to dispel any suspicion.

His early death changed the course of history in the State.[54]

THE FATHER OF BANJARA HILLS

Syed Mohammed Mehdi was born in 1894. After his graduation, he joined the state civil service. He served in many jobs and earned the title of Jung before becoming the commissioner of the Municipal Corporation of Hyderabad from 1937 to 1942. During this period, he improved the civic amenities a great deal. During the Razakar period, 1947-48, he took long leave and remained aloof. He retired in 1949.

In 1927, he bought about 200 acres of lands in Banjara Hills from one Moin Yar Jung who was glad to get rid of this wasteland. Mehdi Nawaz Jung built a 'cave' house largely made of the existing rocks in 1930 and named it *Kohistan*. He exhorted his friends to do likewise offering them land at a nominal price in lots of five to six acres each. He also offered free water supply and electricity for six months. When Rabindranath Tagore visited Hyderabad in 1933, he stayed at the *Kohistan* as his guest. He liked it so much

Nawab Mehdi Nawaz Jung

that he said that if he did not have his Shantiniketan to look after, he would have liked to settle down there. He also composed a poem on *Kohistan* and Banjara Hills and translated it into English himself as follows:

From the distance thou didst appear
Barricaded in rocky aloofness,
Timidly I crossed the rugged path
To find here all of a sudden
An open invitation in the sky,
And friend's embrace in the air,
In an unknown, land the voice that
Seemed ever known,
Revealed to me a shelter of loving intimacy.[55]

Considering the unique nature of the house and the pioneering work that Mehdi Nawaz Jung had done in developing Banjara Hills, some of us proposed in 1983 that the 'Kohistan' should be bought by the government and preserved as a city monument. The then chief minister, NTR agreed to the proposal but by that time, the house had been sold away.

To merely call Mehdi Nawaz Jung the 'father' of Banjara Hills won't be doing justice to his multifaceted personality. After retirement, he took up social work with great gusto. He was instrumental in establishing the Niloufer Hospital for Women & Children, and the Cancer Hospital.

He served as a minister from 1950 to 1960. Thereafter, he was appointed governor of Gujarat. On the completion of his term, he was awarded the Padma Vibushan.

One remarkable thing about the Nawab was his compassion. Amongst other things, he brought up one Hindu boy from a village as a member of his family. Madhusudan rose to become an I.A.S. officer.[56]

A FIELD MARSHAL OF HYDERABAD

Razvi was perhaps the one man for giving Hyderabad its only traumatic experience in its history.

Razvi hailed from Uttar Pradesh and became a lawyer in Latur in Osmanabad, a district of the Hyderabad State. He became a member of the Majlis-e-Ittehad-ul Mussalmeen (Majlis for short) of which Bahadur Yar Jung was the president. The Majlis wanted Hyderabad where the Muslim population was only about twelve percent to be declared an Islamic state.

Razvi became the President of the Majlis in 1946. He fanned communalism in a State, which was generally known for its communal harmony. He delivered highly provocative speeches exhorting Muslims to remember that they had conquered India by sword and that they were destined to rule.

He created a para-military force called '*razakars*' (volunteers). Every *razakar* had to take a pledge that he would lay down his life for the leader and the party and he would fight to the last to maintain the Muslim hegemony in the State. They were given military training and they were armed with sticks, swords, and some with guns. Razvi was the self-appointed Field Marshal of the outfit and wore a khaki uniform.

When India became independent on 15 August 1947, Razvi encouraged the Nizam to make a vain bid to become independent. He declared that the waters of the Bay of Bengal would wash his feet. He also bragged that the Nizam's flag would flutter on the Red Fort at Delhi.

When after negotiations, the Nizam and the Government of India decided to enter a Standstill Agreement in 1947, the *razakars* prevented the Hyderabad delegation from leaving for Delhi for signing the agreement. They also manhandled the prime minister and others. They spread a reign of terror in the State and Razvi issued severe threats to everyone who dared to oppose or even differ from him. A young journalist, Shoebullah Khan was murdered by *razakars* because he wrote in favour of the State's integration with India.

Razvi's power grew and he and his people came to wield increasingly greater influence with the Nizam and the government. The moderate prime minister, Sir Mirza Ismail was hounded out of the State. So was Nawab of Chhattari who had returned to Hyderabad for a second term as Premier in 1947.

In January 1948, Razvi imposed a new government on the State under Mir Laik Ali as prime minister. Many harassed Hindu families left the state for the safety of India.

On the failure of the Standstill Agreement, the Government of India launched the 'Police Action' against Hyderabad on 13 September 1948. Four days later, the Nizam declared an unconditional surrender and General J.N. Choudhuri was appointed the military governor of the State.

All ministers and some prominent leaders of the *Ittehad* including Razvi were taken into custody.

After detailed investigation, three criminal cases were filed against Razvi and six others: the Aland Murder Case, the Shoebullah Khan

Murder Case, and the Bibinagar Dacoity Case. A special tribunal with three judges – one Christian, one Muslim, and one Hindu – was constituted to try the accused. Later, the Government withdrew the Aland Murder case for want of sufficient evidence. Askar Yar Jung, a former member of the State Judicial Committee was appointed the defence counsel along with some others to assist him. At the argument stage, Razvi asked for the removal of the counsels and argued his own case.

On 10 September 1950, the Tribunal held him guilty and awarded him seven years hard labour in the case of the Bibinagar Dacoity Case, and life term in the Shoebullah Khan Murder Case. On appeal in the High Court, the life sentence was quashed but the sentence for seven years hard labour was upheld. The *Razakar* supremo was sent to the Chanchalguda Jail in the city, put in fetters, and asked to cut grass in the jail compound.

Zahid Ali Kamil was a young advocate and an admirer of Razvi. On his own admission, he used to smuggle messages to and from Razvi in the jail. A copy of Razvi's strong letter written to Nehru, the prime minister of India was smuggled out. So was his threat to resort to a hunger strike for the harsh treatment meted out to *razakars* in the jail. To put a stop to smuggling, the

Kasim Razvi

government shifted Razvi to Yervada Jail in Pune in 1954. He served the rest of his term there.

Razvi was released on 11 September 1957. Kamil went to Pune and drove him to his house in Adikmet in his car. Razvi summoned a meeting of the general body of the Majlis. Only about forty of the one hundred and forty members responded to the invitation. At the meeting, he invited leading members of the Party to take up the presidentship of the party. No one came forward. Razvi was so disappointed that he declared that he was willing to offer the job to any male Muslim above the age of twelve! Finally, Abdul Wahid Owaisi was made the president of the Party. Now his grandson, Asaduddin Owaisi is the president of the party. Thereafter, at a press conference, he announced that having no future in India, he would be leaving for Pakistan.

Having settled the issue of party presidentship, Razvi left for Pakistan on 18 September 1957. Kamil flew with him up to Mumbai and saw him off.

Razvi received no reception in Pakistan, not even support, or recognition. He set up his legal practice amongst the refugees from India in Karachi. He died at the age of sixty-seven on 15 January 1970, unwept and unsung in a land far distant from the one which he had dreamt about making an independent Islamic kingdom.[57]

THE SEVENTH NIZAM'S SENSE OF OCCASION

The Seventh Nizam had a sense of occasion. When he went to Aurangabad, he visited the simple and austere grave of the Mughal Emperor Aurangzeb. To underline the fact that he was a descendant of the family of the *subedars* (governors) of the Deccan and the grave was that of the Mughal emperor, he wore the formal uniform of the subedar. The courtiers accompanying him also wore the formal court dress. The attendant of the mausoleum, clad in full Mughal dress recounting all the titles of Aurangzeb, announced to the grave that the subedar of the Deccan, Osman Ali Khan had come to pay his respects. Thereafter the Nizam was admitted to the 'presence' of the simple grave.

In 1935 when he went to Gulbarga for the urs of Khwaja Bande Nawaz

Mir Osman Ali Khan, the Seventh Nizam

Gaisu Daraz, he found that a guard of honour had been mounted for him near the entrance to the shrine. The Nizam peremptorily ordered the guard to be dismissed, saying that he had come to pay respects, not to receive them.

On another occasion, he went to attend a majlis – a religious gathering of Shias in which sermons based on the martyrdom of Husain, the grandson of the Prophet of Islam are delivered. One of the persons there was wearing a *bugloos* – the belt round the waist, which was a part of the court dress of the Nizam. The Nizam pulled him up and asked whether it was God's court he was attending or the Nizam's.

That man removed the *bugloos* promptly.

Once at a sermon in a mosque, the Nizam came a little late. The preacher interrupted his sermon and salaamed the Nizam. The Nizam snubbed him and observed that it was the Nizam who should salaam the preacher because the latter was standing on the pulpit. From that privileged pedestal, he should not salute any man of the world.

On a Friday in 1935, he went for the congregational prayer to a mosque. There, a poet tried to recite a *qasida* – an ode – to him. The Nizam promptly shut him up saying that in a mosque, no paeans to any human being should be sung. 'In the house of God, king and beggar are both equal. Nobody is small or great.'[58]

THE SEVENTH NIZAM & THE RADIO

The Seventh Nizam was reputed to be the richest man of his time. However, his appearance and style of living suggested the contrary. He was indifferent about dress and appearance. It will surprise many to know that he did not own even a radio set.

After India became independent in August 1947, he did not join the new Union. Instead, he decided to become independent. That led to prolonged negotiations between him and the government of India. During the period, the prime minister of India, Nehru, once made a broadcast about Hyderabad. It was proposed that the Nizam should listen to the broadcast. The director of the Radio Deccan (Hyderabad State Radio) was asked to send a radio set to

Mir Osman Ali Khan, the Seventh Nizam

the Nizam's palace, the 'King Kothi'. When the Nizam heard Nehru's voice, he asked where the speaker was sitting. He even looked at the back of the radio set to see whether Nehru was sitting inside the box. The director then explained to him how the speech was being transmitted from Delhi.[59]

Finally, the Police Action against Hyderabad was started on Monday, 13 September 1948. There was hardly any resistance from the Hyderabad forces. The Indian forces reached the outskirts of the city four days later.

On the noon of 17 September, a messenger brought a personal note from the Nizam to K. M. Munshi asking him whether he could see the Nizam at 4 p.m. He had not granted Munshi an interview since his appointment as India's agent general ten months ago.

Earlier, the Nizam had spent the morning in hectic consultations. His premier had seen him twice already. The Nizam had summoned him the previous day and asked for his resignation by the morning of the next day. The cabinet decided to resign forthwith.

As soon as Munshi entered the sitting room, the desolate ruler said, 'The vultures have resigned. I don't know what to do.' He handed him the letter of resignation of Laik Ali, the prime minister. His hands were shaking. He had had this problem for some time, which became pronounced, when he was tense or angry.

Munshi had come to know about the resignation earlier from Laik Ali himself. He said that he was worried about the safety of the citizens. He suggested that General El Edroos should be asked to take steps to preserve law and order in the city.

The Nizam sent for his commander-in-chief and told him accordingly.

Drawing room of Chowmahalla Palace, Hyderabad

Munshi also suggested that the Nizam might make a broadcast welcoming the Police Action and withdrawing his complaint to the Security Council.

'Broadcast! How is that done?' asked the bewildered Nizam.[60]

Munshi explained, and offered to help draft the speech.

It was the Nizam's first visit to the Radio Station. No red carpet was spread for him; no formalities were observed. No music, no anthem was played before or after the broadcast. The speech was in English. Nobody bothered to translate it into Urdu.

That night the city changed a great deal. Many khaki uniforms were discarded, many beards shaved. The shouting, rampaging crowds of *razakars* disappeared magically. The citizens emerged from their cocoons. People of all ages came out in throngs waving the tri-colour of India. Suddenly where there was fear and restraint, now there was life and laughter. There was a general release of tension and a new, quivering anticipation.

Then light began to fade. Vans were going up and down announcing the imposition of the curfew from 7 p.m. to 6 a.m. The crowds began to melt. They hurried to reach their houses in time. There would be celebrations there too.

Soon there was quiet everywhere. Silence and knowledge of security such that the city had not felt for the last many months overcame it. A feeling of peace wrapped it, like a snug comforter. It too slid into sleep – exhausted and relieved.

THE ESCAPE OF A PRIME MINSTER

Mir Laik Ali was the last prime minister of Hyderabad. He was appointed on 1 December, 1947. After the Police Action in September 1948, he was put under house arrest at Begumpet.

His wife and sister, along with a lawyer, Abdul Quvi, prepared a plan for his escape. Quvi made frequent visits to Pakistan and prepared the necessary documents for his flight to Pakistan.

Though police guard was kept at his house, Laik Ali's family members were allowed to visit him. The women used to come in car, which had purdah on the windows according to the custom of those days. Every time the car went out of the house, a female guard used to look into it to check who was inside. In course of time, the security became lax because it was mostly Mrs Laik Ali who was coming in or going out.

Mir Laik Ali, the last prime minister of Hyderabad

One day Mrs Laik Ali announced that her husband had been taken ill. From then on

Laik Ali started behaving like a sick man while his wife started making frantic trips presumably to consult his physician and to bring medicines. Her assumed nervousness and the flurry of traffic made the illness known to everybody including the guards within the house and at the gate. This went on for about a fortnight and even the guards started making enquiries about their important detainee.

Meanwhile it was announced that a marriage was about to be celebrated in the house of one of the relatives of Laik Ali. A lorry came and carried utensils and other things from the house. The *lambadas* started coming daily and performing dance. They were given tips on behalf of Laik Ali and often some sweets were distributed. That provided a welcome diversion to the guards.

On the morning of 3 March, 1950, the maid called for the car saying that the Begum was ready to go to the doctor. When the car pulled in under the portico, Laik Ali quietly slipped into it. The unsuspecting guards were on the other side of the car. Some pillows had been so arranged in his bed as to give the impression that the patient was lying under a blanket. Mrs Laik Ali hid herself in the upper portion of the house. Laik Ali drove straight to his sister's house. From there, he drove to the house of Abdul Quvi in another car. The original car then returned to the house and the maid casually announced that her mistress had come back with medicines. Mrs Laik Ali then emerged from her hiding place and went to her husband's bedroom. She addressed the covered pillows and told them that the physician had changed the medicines. She then pretended to administer the medicine to the patient. The female guard posted at the window did not take any notice of that.

A taxi with curtains was waiting at the residence of Abdul Quvi. Laik Ali and his sister's son joined him and the threesome drove towards

Gulbarga. After they got out of the city, the curtains were drawn and Laik Ali had a look at the countryside for the last time.

A four-berth first class compartment had been booked in the train at Secunderabad with instructions that the passengers would board at Gulbarga. Though there were only three passengers, it was thought prudent to reserve the entire compartment so that nobody else entered the compartment.

The party offered prayers at the shrine of the saint of Gulbarga and then proceeded to the railway station. The train took them to Bombay early in the morning. After bath and breakfast, they left for the airport. Laik Ali flew under the name of Ghulam Ahmed.

Back in Hyderabad, for two days the charade was kept up. Mrs Laik Ali kept on administering medicines to the pillows. Groups of Holi revellers came and were given tips on behalf of the 'ailing' ex-premier. On the next day, Mrs Laik Ali made a number of neat bundles of currency notes. She gave them to her old trusted Arab servant with instructions that they should be disbursed to the named servants on Sunday. She then drove to her brother's house. From there she went to the airport in a purdah car to catch the flight to Bombay. Just short of the airport, the car broke down. The driver got down to push it. From behind came the car of the Inspector General of Police, Jetley. Noticing a purdah car stalled, the chivalrous police chief got down to give it a push!

As Laik Ali boarded the flight to Karachi, his family followed by the ship *S.S. Sabarmati*.

The first news about the escape came from Radio Pakistan. Sri Prakasa who was the High Commissioner of India in Pakistan rang up the home minister of India, Sardar Patel to ask whether Laik Ali had been released. Patel said no and then checked with Hyderabad. It was only then that the administration came to know what a hoax had been played on them.

The government initiated action against the negligent officials. A case for abetting the escape was also filed against Laik Ali's sister, Shoukatunissa Begum. However, the court held that since the Hyderabad Public Safety and Public Interest Regulation and the Hyderabad Penal Code under which Laik Ali had been detained had lapsed after the promulgation of the Constitution of India, the detention itself was illegal. There could therefore be no abetment to a non-existent offence. She and other accused were acquitted.[61]

Laik Ali expired in New York during his morning prayer on 24 October, 1970. His body was taken to Medina for burial.

TABLES TURNED

At the time of the Police Action in 1948, B.P.R. Vithal, an I.A.S. officer of Hyderabad, was a young man of twenty-one. His father Ram Narsu was an assistant professor in the Nizam College. He was an outspoken nonconformist; he did not hesitate to utilise his lectures on British History to justify the aspiration for freedom amongst Indians. The principal, an Englishman called Turner, did not like him, and terminated his services on the ground that the vacancy had ceased to exist.

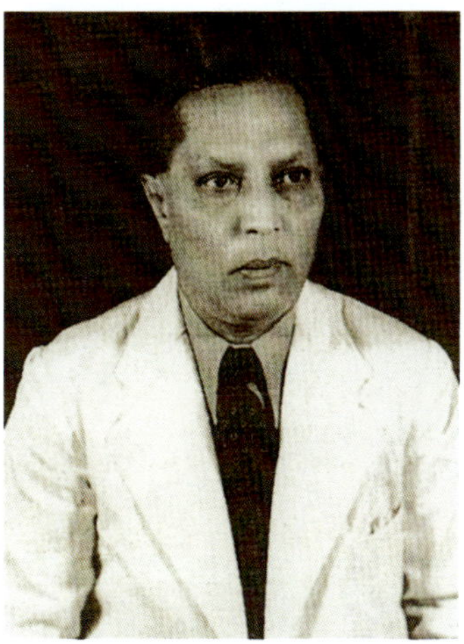

Narsu's wife was a good veena player and that had brought her close to the wife of Hasan Latiff, chief engineer in the government. She was the niece of Sir Akbar Hydari, prime minister of Hyderabad. Due to the death of her father, Hydari had brought her up. She sought Sir Akbar's intercession in the case. He ordered Narsu's immediate reinstatement.

Prof Ram Narsu

Vithal meanwhile had finished his schooling and had joined the Nizam College. A keen sensitive student, Vithal became interested in politics and took part in the Quit India Movement of 1942. He also used to wear khadi clothes. The new principal of the College, Khader Hussain Khan, did not approve of his conduct. He called Narsu and told him about his son's activities and gave him an ultimatum, 'One of you will have to leave the college - you or your son.'

Thereupon Vithal left Hyderabad and joined the Christian College at Madras. He found there comparatively greater freedom to indulge in his youthful politics. There, Vithal started maintaining a journal.

Nizam College, Hyderabad

In and around Hyderabad, tension had started mounting in 1948. Ram Narsu asked a student of his, Makhdoom Ali Khan, who by then had become the treasurer of the Majlis-Ittehad-ul-Mussalmeen, the militant Islamic party, to keep his jewellery and valuables for safe custody – just in case!

'Don't worry, Sir,' replied Makhdoom respectfully, as he took the packet, '*Insha Allah* everything will be alright.'

From the newspapers in Madras in September, Vithal gathered that something serious was in the offing. He therefore decided to pay a visit to his parents. He took the train from Madras on 11th September and found that the train services from Vijayawada to Secunderabad had been cancelled. The train was diverted via Wadi.

There, on the early morning of 12th, three razakars with third class tickets got into Vithal's second-class compartment. No one dared to object. Vithal reached home on the evening of 12 September 1948 to the mild surprise of his family.

The Indian army moved into the Hyderabad State early next morning. His was the last train to enter the State. He thought he was lucky. Now he wondered what would happen and how long he would be stuck in Hyderabad.

A day after the surrender of Hyderabad on 17 September 1948, Vithal went to the telegraph office to send a telegram to his relatives in Vijayawada to inform them that the family was safe. As he stood in a queue, a Muslim youth walked in nonchalantly and stood at the head of the line. Vithal told him that there was a queue and that he should not break it. The young man quietly came back and stood behind Vithal. That night Vithal recorded the incident in his journal and added a comment: 'Can you imagine my doing such a thing a few days ago!'

The same afternoon Makhdoom Ali Khan came to Ram Narsu. He returned the packet of jewellery, which had been in his safekeeping. Then he handed over to Ram Narsu another packet. 'What is this?' the teacher asked.

'Sir, now it is my turn to request you to keep our jewellery in safe custody with you. If you don't mind ...' The gentle teacher's voice choked as he accepted the packet. He patted the young man and said, 'Don't worry. With God's grace, things will be alright.'[62]

'JAI HIND' SAFRANI

When we talk of 'freedom fighters', we generally think of people who were engaged in the struggle for freedom for India within the country. We tend to ignore many other groups who fought for freedom of the country from outside. They represented the radicals in the Congress party who broke away from the main line of the Party because they believed freedom could not be won through peaceful methods and negotiations. Quite a number of them went away from the country and lived a life of exile. A number of such people went to Canada. They married local women, mostly of Hispanic origin – and gave them Indian names. Their progeny is now completely integrated with the local inhabitants.

Another part of the Indian community, which played a crucial role, comprised the Indian expatriates settled in South East Asia. They were the ones who helped the greatest of hero of the armed struggle from abroad – Subhash Chandra

Bose, commonly revered as 'Netaji' in setting up the India National Army. They not only gave moral and material support, but also joined the army in good number. They were from different parts of the country and were drawn from different communities and religions.

One young, colourful, and courageous person from Hyderabad became a freedom fighter by chance. Zain-ul Abideen Hasan, commonly known as Abid Hasan was born to Amir Hasan a district collector and his Iranian wife in 1911 in Hyderabad.

He was sent to Germany to study engineering. During the Second World War, Netaji Subhash Chandra Bose had escaped to Germany to canvass support for an armed struggle to liberate India. Germany was at war with England and so it was in her interest to encourage disaffection in India against the British.

Bose addressed meetings of Indian prisoners of war and other Indians exhorting them to join him in his struggle. Abid met him and inspired by his patriotism and spirit of sacrifice, he told him that he would join him after finishing his studies. Netaji taunted him that if he was worried about small things like that, he could not take up big causes. Stung by that rebuke, Abid Hasan gave up his studies and became his secretary and interpreter.

From then on, he was always by his side. He went with Netaji to Singapore in a German submarine. There, after consultations with the Japanese, Netaji set up the Provisional Government of Free India on 21 October, 1943. He also reorganised the Indian National Army originally established by Mohan Singh, an officer of the British Indian Army.

Abid Hasan became a major in the INA and participated in the march from Burma across the Indian frontier. The army reached Imphal. It was severely handicapped in supplies and armaments and so had to retreat.

Netaji wanted to introduce an Indian form of greeting for his army, and for independent India. Various suggestions came. Abid suggested 'Hello'. Netaji snubbed him. Then he suggested 'Jai Hind'. Netaji liked it and it became the official form of greeting in INA and the revolutionary Indians. Later it was adopted as the official slogan of the country. Netaji also established common kitchens for all soldiers. The Provisional Government of India though fired by idealism, was also riven with squabbles. A major issue was the design of the flag. The Hindus wanted the saffron colour, while the Muslims favoured green. The controversy was beginning to become acute. At that stage, the Hindus gave up their insistence on saffron. Abid Hasan was so touched by the gesture that he decided to add '*Saffrani*' to his name. That is how he came to be known as 'Safrani'.

Indian National Army troops

After the collapse of the INA, Safrani along with others was taken prisoner by the British and jailed in Singapore. Meanwhile, his family back in Hyderabad had no news about him and most – except his mother – gave him up as dead. Then somebody came from Singapore and told her that he had met one Iranian in Singapore. Abid's mother then knew that her son was alive.

After the famous INA trial, all the prisoners were released. In 1946, Abid came back to Hyderabad and joined the Congress Party. However, here too there were rivalries and groupings and he felt disgusted with the group politics in the organisation. He then joined the Bengal Lamp Company and was posted at Karachi. When India attained independence, and Karachi became part of Pakistan, Safrani came back to Hyderabad.

He was taken in the Foreign Service of India in 1948 and served in different diplomatic capacities in China, Switzerland, Iraq, Syria, and Denmark. After his retirement in 1969, he came back to Hyderabad and set up a farm near Dargah Husain Shah Wali.

He remained a bachelor all his life. He adopted three children. One of them is Shahbaz Safrani who is a well-known museologist in the US. Second is Ismet Mehdi, a scholar in Arabic and a former professor at the English & Foreign Languages University. The third is Maleeha. She stays in Toronto in Canada.

Abid Hasan Safrani passed away in 1984. How few of his fellow citizens know about the extraordinary man who embodied all that is rich and valuable in humanity![63]

MEHDI ALI'S IRONY OF FATE

Mehdi Ali was born in 1917 and was selected in the Hyderabad Civil Service in 1941.

In 1948, he was posted as deputy collector at Madhira in Khammam district. The *razakars* were harassing people and even the administration was afraid of them. They would enter trains, loot passengers and otherwise misbehave with them. Once they detained a group of Marwaris and accused them of smuggling gold in their jars, which on search, were found to contain only pickles. The police were on the side of the *razakars* and in spite of the intervention of Mehdi Ali they were harassed for twelve hours before they were allowed to go.

Mehdi Ali's boss was the commissioner of Warangal. He was an Arab named Habeeb Mohammad. He had a good reputation, but after the ascendancy of the *razakars*, he became a fanatic Muslim. He used to declare that he would mix the blood of Hindus with the water of the Bay of Bengal. Mehdi Ali did not like his rabid views, but could do little as he was his subordinate.

The Hindu population was so terror-struck that many moved across into the neighbouring Indian territory.

Under the Nizam, the Arabs guarded the treasury in the district and taluks. They were very good at their job and were fiercely loyal. With deteriorating conditions, they became a law unto themselves. One night they attacked Dindkur village, which was about five kilometres from Madhira. They indulged in loot, arson, and rape. They even removed the *mangala sutras* of women, which are held sacred by every married Hindu woman. The next morning a silent procession of panic-stricken women came to Mehdi Ali to protest about that and demanding action against the guilty persons. The police station was just opposite the residence of Mehdi Ali. At that time the officer in charge of the police station, Habeebullah, was with him.

Mehdi Ali ordered the arrest of the Arabs. The police did nothing. The Arabs freely moved around and waited for the train at the railway station. When the train came, they quietly boarded it with all the loot. Mehdi Ali felt humiliation and pain at the incident. He wrote to the commissioner protesting against the incident and general lawlessness. The commissioner felt enraged that the deputy collector should complain about his brethren in faith. He wrote to the government asking for his immediate transfer.

Kasim Razvi, the president of the Majlis and 'Field Marshal' of *razakars* had also written to Mehdi Ali accusing him of harassing *razakars* unnecessarily. He threatened him with dire consequences unless he changed his ways. Razvi added that if he did not mend his ways, he might soon see 'Warangal'. Mehdi Ali did not understand the meaning of that expression. He learnt later that it meant that he would be sodomised.

Mehdi Ali was promptly transferred. However, luckily for him the Police Action took place soon and Hyderabad became a part of India. He thus escaped the 'dire consequences' threatened by the *razakar* leader.

Soon thereafter, he resumed duty under the new dispensation. When in 1949, his turn came for promotion as collector, he found that his name was missing from the list of eight officers who were promoted. All the promoted officers were Hindus. Thereupon Mehdi Ali contacted Mulla Basith Ali who was one of those who had opposed the policies of the Nizam and had advocated the establishment of responsible government, and accession to India. Both met the prime minister of India, Jawahar Lal Nehru and complained about the injustice and discrimination under the new dispensation. Nehru did not believe it. Basith showed him a copy of the order. On seeing that Nehru was shocked. He immediately rang up Bakhle, the chief civil administrator of Hyderabad and asked him if some officers had recently been promoted as collectors. On an affirmative reply from Bakhle, he asked if there was any Muslim amongst them. None, said Bakhle. He said that a screening was done and no Muslim was included in the list in order to redress the imbalance against the Hindus.

'This is too much and too sudden. Go slow. Let them not feel that any discrimination is being done.'

The list was revised. Three Muslims were included in the new list. Mehdi Ali got his due promotion.

However, he did not advance further. Some years later when his name came up for the next promotion, he was overlooked. He could not imagine the reason. Vohra, an ICS officer who had trained along with him and who was in a high position in the Government of India, told him confidentially that some superior officer of Mehdi Ali had recorded in his confidential roll that 'his loyalties are divided.'

It was a most brutal cut. Such a remark against an officer who had the courage to oppose the *razakars* at the height of their power and who risked his entire career for the sake of justice to the oppressed! Thousands of

Muslims had gone away to Pakistan after the Police Action. He too could have done that. However, he stayed on. He was too shocked to appeal or agitate. He just kept quiet and wondered at the irony of his fate.

When I met him some years ago, he was over eighty. He did not exhibit any trace of bitterness. He had a forgiving smile.[64] He died after a prolonged illness.

A FEUDAL LORD & REVOLUTIONARY

Ravi Narayan Reddy was one of the great heroes of the Freedom Movement in Hyderabad. He was also a colourful and courageous man who sacrificed a great deal for others. A feudal landlord by birth and inheritance, he became a powerful agent for its demise.

He was born in a prosperous jagirdar family in Bollepalle village of Nalgonda district in 1908. As a student in Hyderabad, he took keen interest in sports, scouting, and acting. In 1930, when he was in his Intermediate class, he gave up his studies and joined Mahatma Gandhi's Civil Disobedience Movement.

Ravi was so impressed by Mahatma Gandhi's work for the uplift of Harijans that he went to Wardha and presented his wife's jewellery to Mahatma Gandhi as a donation. When, in 1932 Thacker Bapa established a branch of the All India Harijan Sevak Sangh in Hyderabad Padmaja Naidu was made its president and Ravi its secretary. Next year, on her resignation due to ill health, Ravi became the president and remained in that position for six years. In 1938, he became one of the founder members of the Hyderabad State Congress and, on the government's refusal to lift the ban on it, offered satyagraha in the first batch in 1938. For this, he was imprisoned.

He was also a leading member of the Andhra Mahasabha, which was started in 1928 as a socio-cultural organisation for the Telugu-speaking people of the Madras Presidency. He became its president thrice – in 1941, 1944, and 1945. He transformed it into a vigorous political body. He took up social issues like widow remarriage and literacy. When the Communist Party fixed a ceiling of twenty acres on land holding, Ravi distributed five hundred acres of his share of land to the cultivators, keeping only the prescribed twenty acres for himself. When Mahatma Gandhi passed through Secunderabad in 1934, Ravi donated fifty *tolas* of gold for his cause. However, he was influenced in his political life more by Nehru than Gandhi. Finding the approach of the Congress leaders in the State mild, he joined the Communist Party in 1939 and led the armed struggle of the peasantry of the Telangana area of the State.

Ravi Narayan Reddy

After the Police Action, Ravi and some others believed that the goal had been achieved and the communists should give up the armed struggle. However, there was the Ranadive doctrine propounded at the Second Congress of the Communist Party at Calcutta, in 1948, that called for the continuation of the armed struggle. Consequently, there was confusion in the ranks of the party as to the future course of action.

However, the imposition of the ban on the Communist Party three days after the Police Action made the decision for them. Ready to come out in the open, Ravi and his comrades were once again driven to their hideouts. They reverted either to their previous lifestyle - spending their days underground, or in prison. Released days before the first General Elections of 1952, Ravi contested for both the Parliament as well as the State Assembly. His was elected to both. He polled the highest number of votes for the Parliament in the country surpassing even Nehru. His opponents did not get a single vote. In Nalgonda district, his party won all the fourteen Assembly seats though he addressed only two meetings.

In the second General Elections of 1957, due to a taunt of the Congress for having defeated the People's Democratic Front - a group of left parties under which banner the Communists had fought the election - he was asked to contest for the State Assembly. His opponent was his wife's elder brother V. Ramachandra Reddy, who was the first to donate hundred acres of land and thus to launch Vinoba Bhave's Bhoodan Movement. He lost to Ravi by 8,000 votes.

Ravi was an atheist. He never visited temples but did not stop the members of his family from doing so.

He was one of the strong proponents of the movement for an integrated Telugu-speaking state. A good deal of the credit for the formation of Andhra Pradesh, therefore, must go to him.

A legend in his lifetime, this veteran of the armed struggle, passed away in glory on 7 September, 1991. His last words were addressed to Ch. Rajeshwara Rao from whom he enquired what had happened to the cases of the pension of some of the freedom fighters, which he had canvassed.

In his will, he said that his wife should not remove her bangles or her kumkum, the vermilion mark on her forehead, as widows customarily do. He also enjoined upon his children not to immerse his ashes in the Ganga or some other river, but to scatter them over the crops in his fields.[65]

THE OMNIPOTENT RESIDENT

The British Residents appointed in Indian princely states have been called a case of indirect rule of India by the British. While the superficial frills of royalty were left with the rajas and nawabs, real power lay with the British government, which was discreetly exercised by the Residents. They watched, they advised, and if needed they ordered the puppets to dance to their tune.

The Resident controlled the affairs of the Nizam in all spheres through servile dewans. After the Mutiny of 1857 when the Residency in Hyderabad was unsuccessfully attacked by a mob, another Residency was built at Bolarum in the heart of the first cantonment in India, which afforded better protection to him. The Army Commander also reported to him and so he was enormously powerful. The post of the Resident of Hyderabad was coveted by every British officer in India.

Every prime minister of Hyderabad, on his appointment, called on the Resident. The latter returned the call. We have a detailed account of the protocol observed on the occasion when the Nawab of Chhattari became prime minister of Hyderabad for the second time on 9 June, 1947. He called on the Resident, C. G. Herbert, on 30 June at 11 a.m. A guard of honour

Premier of Hyderabad Nawab of Chhattari and Resident A.C. Lothian signing the rendition agreement of Secunderabad 1945 *(courtesy Salar Jung Museum)*

of hundred regular members under a viceroy's commissioned officer was drawn up in front of the Residency steps. Thereafter the premier was received by an under secretary who led him up the steps. The Resident met him at the top of the steps and led him to the drawing room while the under secretary followed. After some time, on a signal, a jamadar brought a tray containing four bottles of *ittar* and a paan and gave it to the under secretary who rose, touched it, and helped the jamadar to present it to the premier. When the premier left, the Resident accompanied him up to the top of the steps whence the under secretary conducted him to his car. A guard of honour again was presented to the premier on his departure. The time and date of the return call by the Resident was intimated by the secretary of the Resident to the chief secretary whom the former addressed as 'My dear Razvi'. The Resident corresponded only with the prime minister, often through his secretary. The latter addressed the prime minister as 'My dear

Nawab Sahib'. The highest officers of the Nizam wrote only to the secretary of the Resident. This shows the authority and position of the Resident of Hyderabad. The Resident stayed in the Residency either at Hyderabad or at the cantonment until 1933.

After that, having retroceded the Hyderabad Residency and the Troop Bazaar to the Nizam, he moved to Trimulgherry in the cantonment. That building is now named Rashtrapati Nilayam and is used as the southern residence of the President of India.

In all, from 1779 to 1947, there were fifty-nine Residents. The sixth Resident, J.A. Kirkpatrick, (1798-1805) who negotiated the Subsidiary Alliance in 1798, may be considered the founder of the cantonment of

Residency House, Bolarum. Now used as Rashtrapati Nilayam

Secunderabad. A. C. Lothian, (1942-45) who signed the Rendition Treaty in 1945, could be credited with the creation of the civilian city. Sir W. P. Barton (1924-27) and T. H. Keyes (1927-30) are remembered in Secunderabad for a number of educational and other institutions named after them. Keyes established the Town Improvement Trust and provided modern drainage and sewerage system in the twin city.[66]

The last Resident, C. G. Herbert, was invited to a farewell tea party by the Nizam on 14 July 1947.

WORLD'S LARGEST ONE MAN'S COLLECTION

Yusuf Ali Khan was a scion of the Salar Jang family. His grandfather and father had been prime ministers of Hyderabad. However, his father, Laik Ali Khan was dismissed in less than three years of service in 1887. He died of frustration at the age of twenty-seven.

Yusuf's young widowed mother was very possessive of him. She did not approve of any woman whom Yusuf fancied for marriage. He therefore remained a bachelor.

In 1912 Yusuf Ali Khan was appointed prime minister by the Seventh Nizam and given the title of Salar Jung III. However, within two years the young prime minister lost his job. He was naturally very depressed and his mother was worried whether her husband's history would repeat itself in the case of her son also. She sent for the family physician, Dr Hunt, who examined Salar Jung III and found that he was suffering from nothing except depression.

He discreetly suggested to Yusuf Ali Khan that to escape boredom he might consider collecting art objects, which incidentally, he said, would be good business too. The Salar Jung family had a lot of heirlooms and antiques lying in various places. They included gifts from various personages

from all over the world given to his father, grandfather, and others before them. Salar Jung III then started classifying them and took the help of his family jeweller at Mumbai for evaluation of the foreign jewellery. He also employed the local auctioneers as agents for collection of antiques. When the word about Salar Jung's interest reached Christie's and Sotheby's of London, they started treating him as a valuable customer.

Sometimes Salar Jung helped some needy people by buying things from them even though they might not qualify strictly for acquisition. Salar Jung also started collecting objects during his foreign travels. In course of time over 43,000 art objects, 47,000 books, and 8,000 manuscripts and many European paintings came into his possession. However, before he could set up the museum he died in March 1949 at the age of sixty.

In 1951, an agreement was reached between government and some 114 parties who laid claim to his estate to set up a museum in the hereditary residence of Salar Jung called Dewan Deodi. It was a sprawling 250-year old 100-room mansion in the old city.

An Act of a Parliament was passed in 1961, naming the museum as an institution of national importance. As the Dewan Deodi was in a dilapidated condition, a new building was constructed and the museum moved into the new building in 1968. Subsequently, in 2000, the museum added two more buildings on either side of the central building. The collection was also categorised on a regional basis and displayed the European materials in the Western Block and Eastern & Far Eastern materials in the Eastern Block. The museum is a unique one-man collection in the world and about 4,000 persons on an average visit it every day.[67] No visitor's tour of Hyderabad is complete without visiting Yusuf's House of Wonder.

Facing Page: Yusuf Ali Khan, Salar Jung III

STALIN'S ORDERS ON THE RED REVOLT

The Communist Party in Hyderabad wanted the overthrow of the existing feudal regime. In September 1947, their leaders gave a call to their cadres to 'intensify the liberation struggle and to take to arms'.

They acquired arms by all sorts of means including looting of police stations, army posts and landlords. Special squads called '*dalams*' were constituted and the volunteers vowed to fight to death.

At its height before the Police Action, the communists in the Nalgonda district alone had '*liberated*' over 2000 villages. All landholdings in excess of two hundred acres were taken over from the landlords and distributed amongst the landless. Wages of agricultural labourers were raised. Toddy tappers were given palmyra trees at low price. Villagers contributed voluntary labour to dig canals, tanks, and wells for irrigation. Wood was made available free from the government forestland for making agricultural implements and carts. People's courts were constituted. Widow remarriages were organised; night schools were set up for promoting adult literacy. A new social and political consciousness was created amongst the people.

Facing Page: Salar Jung Museum, Hyderabad

The communists controlled vast stretches of countryside. The people in villages welcomed them and, at one time, it seemed that a 'red revolution' was in the offing.

Hyderabad became a part of India on 17 September 1948. Three days later, the Communist Party was banned again. Some of the members of the Party had already emerged in the open and others were preparing to do so. Inside the Party, a debate was raging whether the insurrection should be abandoned or carried on. Most of those who had been in the thick of the struggle were in favour of giving it up because the country had become free and the *jagirdari* system had been abolished in Hyderabad. However, some leaders, sitting at a distance, favoured its continuance. Amongst them was Ranadive, the general secretary of the Party, who held that the country had not yet become free. Nehru was an agent of the Anglo-American imperialists and so the struggle must continue.

Meanwhile the mood of the peasantry had also changed. The civil administration had provided for the protection of the rights of tenants. What was there to fight for now? The new regime seemed to be going on the right lines. When Chandra Rajeshwara Rao, who later rose to be the head of the communist party, sought refuge in a field of his old hosts, the tribals in Damelakonta in Karimnagar, he perceived a certain lack of warmth on their part. As of old, he plucked some ears of millet and started roasting them to appease his hunger. Suddenly, he noticed that the tribals were looking around with shifty eyes. Instinct told him that he had been betrayed to the army. In fact, the soldiers were closing in on the field. He jumped, bolted away, and was barely able to escape.[68]

The tribals begged the *dalams* not to come to them. There was no protection against the army because the comrades did not stay in the village as they used to earlier. The police and the military followed their visit. It was then that the saying gained currency in the countryside that 'the communists were the lords of the night, and the police the lords of the day'.

The Indian army started pressing hard against the communists by the end of 1950. In 1951, they adopted the ruthless 'Briggs Plan', which had been implemented earlier in Malaysia. According to that, the army would burn the tribal villages, collect all the tribals, and set them up in barbed-wired encampments. While they were allowed to go to the forest to collect the produce, an adult male member of each family was kept as a hostage to ensure their return. Thus, having isolated and trapped the guerrillas, they set out to annihilate them. The crunch was acute.

It had been easy to fight the Nizam's outfit; that was not the case with the Indian army. In a matter of three days, the communists lost two hundred of their men. It was decided by the leadership to go underground. Most retreated into the forests of Godavari and Karimnagar districts.

When the party leadership could not settle the issue of the continuance of the armed struggle, a delegation was sent to Moscow in 1951 to discuss the issue with the leaders of Comintern (International Communism). The delegation consisted of four leaders. Dange and Ajoy Ghosh were in favour of the withdrawal. Chandra Rajeshwara Rao and Basavapunniah were against the proposal - or not quite sure.

Stalin

The four men stayed in Moscow for six months. They had a number of meetings with the top leadership. Finally, they met Stalin in the Kremlin. Molotov, Malenkov, and Suzlov were also present. A stack of documents had been sent to Moscow and translated into Russian.

Stalin asked for a map of the area in question. A map of India and another of southern peninsula were spread before him. He filled up his pipe, lighted it, and asked:

'Is there a foreign country close to the area?'

'No, Comrade.'

'Is there a port from which you can escape?'

'No.'

'Is there any other sanctuary where you can take refuge?'

'No, Sir.'

Stalin took a deep pull at his pipe, pushed the maps away to clear his table, and observed, 'In the circumstances it would seem difficult for you to sustain the resistance.'[69]

As a result of his verdict, the party announced its withdrawal of the armed struggle on 21 October 1951. However, by that time, the Government of India had all but crushed the resistance physically.

SOME BED-TIME STORIES

THE AMAZONS OF THE NIZAM

The Second Nizam had two battalions of women soldiers - numbering 2,000. They were called 'Zaffar Paltan' or the 'victorious platoon'. The female soldiers were called 'guardnees' - feminine of the English word 'guard'. They were dressed like the British soldiers of old and were regularly trained according to the French system. They accompanied the Nizam in the battle of Khadla with the Marathas in 1795. Their main job was to mount guard in the harem and to accompany the zenana. That was probably the first women's brigade in the world.

In course of time, it ceased to exist, the supervision of the seraglio being best done by eunuchs according to the age-old practice. The eunuchs were specially selected for this job because they were incapable of any 'mischief' with the women of the harem. They ensured the observation of the code of morality. However, these Amazons must have faded gradually.

In 1861, the Assistant Resident at Hyderabad, Briggs, saw six of those girls at the residence of the Paigah noble, Rafiuddin. While doing a drill for him, they giggled, shy and bashful like any other girls. At that time,

Amazons of Hyderabad – The Nizam's all women Brigade

they looked quite unmilitary-like with crumpled trousers, with chappals instead of shoes for footwear and wielding bamboo staves.[70]

MUTINY AND THE HOROSCOPE

Philip Meadows Taylor was the regent of the minor Raja Venkatappa Naik of Shorapur estate during 1830s. A pundit showed him the horoscope of the infant prince and gave his prediction that he would die in his twenty-fourth year and his estate would be forfeited. At that time Taylor simply laughed it off and in course of time even forgot about it. The young boy had been brought up by Taylor and had shown promise of becoming a good ruler of his estate, loyal to the British.

During the Mutiny of 1857, his tribe of Beydurs abetted him and it attacked a small force of the English sent to reinforce Captain Campbell's garrison. This attack was repulsed and thereupon the Raja fled to Hyderabad. For his part in the rebellion, the Raja was sentenced to death.

Philip Meadows Taylor, British Regent, Shorapur estate

Since Taylor had brought him up, he had developed affection for him. He therefore appealed for mercy. The Resident, in the maximum exercise of his authority, commuted it to transportation for life. On further consideration, the Governor-General reduced it to confinement for four years at Chennai.

The Raja's wives celebrated this show of mercy by the English, and, since he was permitted to keep them with him, they made ready to join him. However, after only one-day's journey towards his destination, the Raja shot himself dead.

The gloomy prediction of the astrologer of Shorapur was thus fulfilled.[71]

THE DEATH OF SALAR JUNG I

Salar Jung I became the dewan of Hyderabad at the young age of twenty-three and remained in that job for thirty long years. He reformed every aspect of the administration of the medieval state of Hyderabad and made it into a modern administration. This he did by bringing into Hyderabad a large number of English educated

Sir Salar Jung I *(courtsey Abhisek Patel)*

Indians from the then British India. He was undoubtedly the greatest prime minister of the state.

He crushed the flare up against the British in Hyderabad during the Mutiny of 1857. For this he earned the gratitude of the British. He travelled extensively both in India and abroad.

It seemed that the thought of death was always present in the mind of Sir Salar Jung I. Whenever he proceeded on a longish trip, he always carried with him a coffin and the paraphernalia of funeral should he pass away during the course of his journey.

In the event, he died at home. Sir Salar Jung was interested in astrology and fortune-telling. He had some retainers who were competent in these. One of them was Pandit Mohan Lal. He had an appointment to meet the dewan on the evening of 8 February 1883. After finishing his work, the dewan summoned the Pandit. He asked him to draw his horoscope at that time. The astrologer indicated prosperity and success in store for him. The prime minister examined the horoscope, smiled and then asked the expert teasingly, 'But Pandit ji, the house meant for life is empty.' The Pandit tried to explain away the matter and after a while was allowed to depart.

The astrologer came running to Server-ul-Mulk, his godfather, woke him up, and told him the whole story. Server-ul-Mulk was angry with him that he had disturbed him for such a small matter. The astrologer said that he hoped his horoscope was wrongly cast.[72]

Sir Salar Jung expired later that night. The verdict was death due to cholera but his French governess, M. Gaigaud swore that he was poisoned.

JAGIRDARS COLLEGE

The feudal state of Hyderabad had about 2,600 jagirs of all sizes – from the largest under the Nizam himself followed by the Paigahs and then down the line. It was an oppressive system and there was a struggle for their abolition as part of the freedom movement in Hyderabad. There were over 200 taxes levied on the subjects in these estates. The following are some of them listed by late K.V. Ranga Reddy, an advocate, freedom fighter, and finally deputy chief minister of Andhra Pradesh:

- If there was a birth in the jagirdar's family, a Cradle Tax was levied.
- Upon a death in his family, an Ash (Funeral) Tax.
- Upon the purchase of a horse, a Horse Tax.
- Upon the purchase of motorcar, a Motor Tax.
- Upon a marriage in the family, a Marriage Tax.

Jagirdars College. Now Hyderabad Public School

- Upon the Navaratri festival, a Navaratri Tax. Same with other festivals.
- If the jagirdar went on a tour, there was a Tour Tax.

The taxes varied from jagir to jagir and there were occasional attempts by the state government to rationalise them.[73] After the integration of the state into India, all jagirs were abolished by the military governor in 1949.

Towards the beginning of the second decade of the rule of Nizam VII, the director general of the revenue department of the state, H. Wakefield suggested the establishment of a college for the education of the sons of the jagirdars and nobles of Hyderabad. It was to be an exclusive institution on the lines of the Eton and the Harrow Public Schools of England. The land for this institution was given by lady Vicar-ul-Umra from her jagir of 1679 acres given to her by her husband for her *Pan Ka Kharcha* - (literally expenses for Pan - betel leaves; in other words for miscellaneous petty expenses).

Every jagirdar contributed two percent of his annual income for the fund for its establishment and maintenance. The first son was admitted free while others had to be paid for.

Completed in 1923, it was a residential school and became the most prestigious educational institution in Hyderabad.

Its architectural style became a hallmark of Hyderabadi architecture of the early 20th Century. In 1951, its name was changed to the Hyderabad Public School and, the jagirdari system having been abolished, it was thrown open to commoners. From an exclusive Boys School, it has become co-educational and has reservations for scheduled caste and backward classes. Despite the emergence of many new public schools, Hyderabad Public School, with its vast playgrounds and other amenities and reasonable fees, retains its premier position.[74]

Princess Niloufer at a function *(Courtesy Abhishek Patel)*

THE BARREN PRINCESS

The second son of the Seventh Nizam, Muazzam Jah, was married to Princess Niloufer, the niece of the last caliph of Islam. She was a stunning beauty. While the wife of the Prince of Berar, Durru Shehvar, bore two sons, Niloufer was childless.

Once she went to Ajanta to see the famous caves. To mark the occasion, the local administration there requested her to plant a fruit sapling in the garden opposite the caves.

The princess obliged but said philosophically, 'Why do you ask me to plant this sapling? It will not bear any fruit.' She was referring to her own infertility.[75]

AFTER THE UNIVERSITY

The Osmania University was established in 1919 and was named after Mir Osman Ali Khan, the Seventh Nizam. When it moved into the grand new building in 1938, it had the best architecture, which combined both the Hindu and Muslim elements in an attractive blend. It also had the distinction of being the first university in India to have an Indian language as the medium of instruction, Urdu. The physical amenities provided to students in the university were of a high order. The hostels were furnished generously and the common rooms had sofa sets. The scale of amenities was so good that it stood out in comparison to what was available in other Indian universities. Professors coming from other Indian universities when accommodated there felt that they compared favourably with the contemporary posh hotels. Sibte Hasan, who had come from the North, met Makhdoom Mohiuddin, who was studying in the University at that time. Hasan asked him, "Students live in such luxury here. What will they do after leaving the university?"

Makhdoom replied with his typical laugh, "Become clerks in the government."

Makhdoom rose to international fame later as a poet and a communist leader.[76]

Makhdoom Mohiuddin

Arts college, Osmania University

REPULSING THE ARMY ATTACK

Hyderabad was completely unprepared to face the Indian army when India launched the Police Action in 1948. The false propaganda by the razakars and their leaders about the might of their own and the weakness of the Indian army had lulled the common man into a false complacency.

Just before the brief operation, a worried civilian officer of Hyderabad posted in one of the frontier taluks near Vijayawada sought the advice of Yamin Zuberi, minister of Local Government, and Labour about how to cope with the Indian army, if ever an attack took place.

'Very simple,' replied the minister earnestly, 'Get hold of an ass. Tie a bunch of crackers on its tail, set it afire, and push it towards the enemy. They will all panic and run away.'

Luckily, this was never tried. The Indian army was not trained to face such ingenious tactics.[77]

DISCONNECTION OF NIZAM'S PHONES

Syed Naqi Bilgrami was the secretary of the communications ministry of the government of Hyderabad. Railways, airline, road transport, posts, telegraphs, and telephones were all under him. After the Police Action, all the departments except telephones were taken over by the Government of India.

A fortnight after the Police Action, Bilgrami received an urgent message from King Kothi. The Nizam wanted to see him. Bilgrami asked General Choudhuri, the Military Governor, for permission to do so. The two had known each other from earlier days and were on good terms. The General said, 'Do go and see him. He will ask you about his telephones.'

'What about telephones?'

'They have been disconnected.'

'Why?'

'Because the old man violated his undertaking not to make any calls outside the State.'

His secretary Hosh Yar Jung had made calls from the King Kothi to Sir Mirza Ismail in Bangalore and they had been intercepted. General Choudhuri thereupon ordered all King Kothi phones to be cut off.

'What should I tell the Nizam then?' asked Bilgrami.

'Tell him the reason for the disconnection. And, if he promises to honour the undertaking, restore the connections.'

'Should I get anything in writing?'

'No,' said the military governor, 'his word should be enough. He must have been chastened by now.'

Bilgrami put on his formal dress – *sherwani* and *bugloos* – and presented himself before His Exalted Highness. The Nizam was in tears. 'Look at what they have done to me!' he whimpered, 'If you had been there it could never have happened.'

'What is the matter, *Ala Hazrat*?' Bilgrami pretended as if he knew nothing.

'The wires, the wires. They have cut them off,' he pointed to the phone next to him. Bilgrami explained the reason. Nizam was furious with Hosh Yar Jung. That was only pretence because the calls could have been made only at his instance.

'What should I do now?' asked the crushed Nizam.

'I shall do the needful, Your Exalted Highness. But please tell your staff to be careful in future.'

'Should I give a letter to the *Fouji* General?'

'No, *Ala Hazrat*. That won't be necessary.'

The lines were restored immediately.[78]

Syed Naqi Bilgrami, secretary, communications ministry of Hyderabad

QUEEN'S WEDDING ANNIVERSARY

The Holy Trinity Church in Bolarum in Secunderabad was built in 1846 with a donation from Queen Victoria and a gift of land by the Nizam. The church has a small organ, which was shipped from Europe.

The steeple bell was cast in a foundry in Secunderabad.

In 1983 Queen Elizabeth II and

Prince Philip during their tour of India, paid a visit to Hyderabad. On their wedding anniversary, they were expected to visit the the Holy Trinity Church and the local military band spent many hours practising the tune of `Here comes the bride' to be played when the royal couple would walk down the Church aisle.

As it happened, Prince Philip went away for a hunt and so did not accompany the Queen. She came alone and the band therefore had to change the tune suddenly. It played the next best tune the master knew – 'Colonel Boogey March.'

The Queen did not betray her amusement.[79]

'UNSEATING' THE NIZAM

The renowned musician Pandit Jasraj's father, Pandit Moti Ram, was the court musician of the Sixth Nizam. Pandit Jasraj comes every year to

Queen Elizabeth II at the Qutb Shahi Tombs in 1983. The author is on far right

Hyderabad and holds a festival of music for three days in the memory of his father and brother.

Once, on 6 September, 1998, there was a private sitting at the residence of one of his staunch admirers, Sunita Budhiraja. One of the songs he sang was in Rag Yaman with the following wording:

Aane naa dooongi laaj Ali par
Hasan Hussain par vari jaoon

By way of introduction, he narrated the following incident:

Once an evening of music was being organised for the Sixth Nizam. The court officials put a chair for the Nizam opposite the platform for the singer. Pandit Moti Ram suggested that the Nizam should sit on the floor. The officials said that was a scandalous suggestion. Panditji then said, 'You wait and see. I shall make him sit on the floor.'

When the session started, he started with the song mentioned above. Since it is in praise of the Prophet's son-in-law, Ali, and his grandsons Hasan and Hussain, the Nizam quietly left his chair and sat down on the floor.

Pandit Jasraj

JINNAH'S MEETING WITH THE SEVENTH NIZAM

In 1946 the Seventh Nizam decided to appoint Sir Mirza Ismail as his prime minister. The Majlis-e-Ittehad-e-

Mussalmeen in Hyderabad and the Muslim League in British India did not favour him. M.A. Jinnah, president of the League telegraphically advised the Nizam against the proposal. The Nizam did not respond. Jinnah then sought a meeting with him.

Jinnah entered the room smoking a cigar and sat down in front of the chair with outstretched legs. The offended Nizam exploded: 'You know who I am? Is it the way to behave towards the Nizam?' Flabbergasted, Jinnah immediately threw away the cigar, withdrew his legs and apologised. The Nizam asked him, 'What do you want to tell me?' Jinnah had hardly uttered a few words against the proposal when the Nizam interrupted him, 'I do not want any outside interference in my affairs. I can look after my interests and those of my people.'

Thereupon Jinnah said that in that case the Muslim League would not extend any support to him in Hyderabad, or in the Constituent Assembly. The threat made matters worse. The Nizam retorted that he did not care. He did not need his help.

Jinnah then said something about constitutional reforms. The Nizam cut him short saying that he was a busy person and could not discuss details with him. 'You can go and meet the concerned minister.' Then he asked, 'Anything else?'

'No,' replied Jinnah curtly.

'Then good bye.'

Old-timers swore they had never heard Nizam in such temper.[80]

LAST DAYS OF THE LAST NIZAM

In February 1967, the Nizam was taken ill and as usual was treated by his physician of the Unani system. The illness was attributed to various causes, like flu or broncho-pneumonia but there was no proper diagnosis. He would have none of the allopathic treatment. On 18 February, he had a relapse. Still his daughter Shahzadi Pasha would not allow any allopathic doctors to examine her father. The same afternoon three of his wives left for the *hajj* pilgrimage. It was the first time they were travelling by air. So an official was sent to accompany them. The Nizam bade them good-bye and told them they would not see him alive on their return. They upbraided him for uttering such inauspicious words and said they would pray for his early recovery. The next day he became very weak.

The Seventh Nizam in old age

On the 20th, when he could no longer protest, Dr Waghray, his medical advisor, summoned three allopathic doctors, Bankat Chander, G.P. Ramayya, and Syed Ali, to his bedside. The bedroom was dark and filthy. Dr Ramayya felt he was entering a 'dungeon'. He took the Nizam's pulse and found he had fever. The physicians found his condition deteriorating. However, Shahzadi Pasha would not allow them to give any injection, much less take a sample of his blood for test. On 22 February, a cable was sent to his grandson and designated successor Mukarram Jah in London, informing him about the Nizam's serious condition. An anxious crowd had gathered outside the King Kothi. Police reinforcements were brought in to keep them in check.

On the 22nd, Mukarram Jah and his younger brother Mufakkam Jah arrived from London and met their ailing grandfather. The Nizam was glad to see Mukarram Jah and held him close. However, he could not speak. He had already become unconscious. That day the doctors put him on oxygen.

On the night of the 23rd, a nurse was seen coming out of the Nizam's bedroom with an oxygen cylinder. She seemed to have made a gesture of wiping her eyes. The intelligence man on duty standing at a distance thought she had wiped her tears. He drew his own conclusions from that.

Syed Hashim Ali, director of protocol of the state government, had already drafted an obituary note for the Gazette Extraordinary, which would be issued on the death of the Nizam. Earlier, he along with Prahlad Singh, the commissioner of police and Brigadier Ferris, the sub-area commander of the army, had visited King Kothi to finalise the arrangements for the funeral, which seemed imminent.

The next morning, Hashim Ali and Prahlad Singh visited King Kothi again. The Nizam was sinking. It was only a matter of hours. The officials of the government and those of the King Kothi met at the office of Taraporewala, the Nizam's financial advisor. Prince Mukarram Jah also walked in. Hashim told him that they had come to discuss the arrangements in the event of the Nizam's demise. Mukarram Jah said that it was their custom not to announce the death for three days. Hashim replied that it was probably necessary in earlier times because the issue of succession was disputed. Now that he had already been notified as the successor, it did not seem necessary to do that. In any case, the people would know from the Press. Then there was the question of keeping the body in state. Mukarram Jah was opposed to that idea. It had never been done before for any Nizam. Again, Hashim said that there would be crowds of people who would want to see his face and pay their last respects. Mukarram Jah demurred, but finally agreed on both the points.

The end came at twenty-two minutes past one in the afternoon on 24 February, 1967. Dr Ramayya put his stethoscope on the chest of the Nizam and pronounced him dead. He certified the death due to cardiac failure. The richest man of the world passed away without any modern treatment. Prince Mukarram Jah, his younger brother, their mother, Nizam's stepbrother Basalat Jah, the three doctors, and some other members of the household were all by his bedside. An hour later, the body was brought out and kept below the *shamiana* specially erected in the courtyard of King Kothi. The crowds started breaking into the compound and the police formed a cordon and asked them to form a queue to file past in an orderly manner.

A touch of bathos was provided when the Prince of Berar came to the King Kothi at 3 p.m. He ambled up to the body of his father and touched his feet as a mark of respect. When he came out, a journalist asked him for some comment on the sad event. The Prince looked blankly at Abdul Mannan, a retired deputy secretary of the Finance Department, whom he

Funeral Procession of Mir Osman Ali Khan, the last Nizam *(Courtesy: Abhishek Patel)*

had appointed his secretary and who was standing by his side. As if on a cue, Abdul Mannan began to whisper into his ears and the Prince kept on repeating whatever Abdul Mannan said, 'He was a great man. He was the architect of modern Hyderabad. He established the Osmania University. He separated the executive from the judiciary. He implemented a number of reforms in the administration. The people of Hyderabad will never forget him...etc.' and then after a while when the secretary thought he had said enough, he whispered to ask the Prince, 'Anything more?' The Prince, thinking that it was a part of the prompting, repeated loudly: 'Anything more?'

The Nizam's second son, Prince Muazzam Jah, did not attend the funeral. He was sleeping off his nocturnal vigil. When an aide tried to wake him up and told him about the Nizam's demise, he mumbled with closed eyes, 'Don't bring such unpleasant news so early in the morning.' Then he turned on his side and resumed his sleep.[81]

Early next morning the body was given a bath. A prayer was said and a brand-new, unnumbered ambulance van started cutting through thousands of mourners wending its way to the Mecca Masjid. There a prayer was held. The police wanted to mount a loudspeaker in the mosque to appeal to the crowds for order. The *imam* of the mosque objected to that saying, 'It would desecrate the sacred precincts because it carried the voice of Satan.' That created difficulties in controlling the crowds. There was confusion outside. The prayers over, the body was brought out and placed in a gun carriage. An estimated crowd of 200,000 people formed the procession. People hung from their balconies and occupied every possible vantage point to be a witness to the historic moment.

Another view of the funeral procession showing the thronging crowds *(Courtesy: Abhishek Patel)*

The gun carriage reached the Judi Mosque at 11 a.m. It was built by the Nizam in memory of his son Jawad. The Arab guards and the Sikh *paltan* dressed in the uniform of the private estate of the Nizam, barefoot and holding naked swards, took charge of the body of their supreme commander. The members of the family gave shoulder to the coffin. A detachment of the police sounded the last post and a unit of the army reversed their arms in their last mournful salute to the Nizam.

The body was taken out from the coffin and two old servants of the Nizam, Manzoor Ali, and Muhammad Bin Habel lowered it into the grave dug by the side of the grave of his beloved mother and his son, as the crowd droned *Allah-ho-Akbar*. The Nizam's sons, daughter, grandsons, stepbrother, and others threw a fistful of earth each gently into the grave. Mir Osman Ali Khan, the seventh and the last Asaf Jah, was returned to earth.[82]

One Muhammad Ali Beg issued an advertisement in the papers with his own tribute. He quoted the first line of his famous couplet:

Salateen-e-salf ho gaye nazar-e-ajal Osman,

Mussalmaanon kaa teri saltanat se hai Nishaan Baaqi.

(Sultans of old have been claimed by Death.

By your rule Muslims are now identified.)

'And now,' said the advertisement, 'the writer of this line himself has joined them.' Beg did not omit to mention that he was a resident of Charminar and his phone number was 41019.

With the passing away of the Seventh Nizam, an era ended in Hyderabad. Its break with the past was now complete.

CHIEF MINISTERS OF HYDERABAD

1.	General J. M. Choudhuri, Military Governor	1948-49
	(D. S. Bakhle, ICS, Chief Civil Administrator)	1948-49
2.	M. K.Vellodi, ICS, Chief Civil Administrator	1949-52
3.	B. Ramakrishna Rao, Chief Minister	06-03-1952 – 01-11-1956

CHIEF MINISTERS OF ANDHRA PRADESH

1.	Neelam Sanjeeva Reddy	01-11-1956 – 11-11-1960
2.	Damodaram Sanjivayya	11-1-1960 – 12-3-1962
3.	Neelam Sanjeeva Reddy	12-3-1962 – 29-2-1964
4.	Kasu Brahmananda Reddy	29-2-1964 – 30-9-1971
5.	P.V. Narasimha Rao	30-9-1971 – 18-1-1973
	President's Rule	18-1-1973 – 10-12-1973
6.	Jalagam Vengala Rao	10-12-1973 – 06-3-1978
7.	Dr Marri Channa Reddy	06-3-1978 – 11-10-1980
8.	Tanguturi Anjaiah	11-10-1980 – 24-2-1982
9.	Bhavanam Venkatram	24-2-1982 – 20-9-1982
10.	K. Vijayabhaskara Reddy	20-9-1982 – 09-01-1983
11.	N.T. Rama Rao	09-01-1983 – 16-8-1984
12.	Nadendla Bhaskara Rao	16-8-1984 – 16-9-1984
13.	N.T. Rama Rao	16-9-1984 – 09-3-1989
14.	Dr Marri Channa Reddy	03-12-1989 – 17-12-1990
15.	N. Janardhana Reddy	17-12-1990 – 09-10-1992
16.	K. Vijayabhaskara Reddy	09-10-1992 – 12-12-1994
17.	N.T. Rama Rao	12-12-1994 – 01-9-1995
18.	N. Chandrababu Naidu	01-9-1995 – 13-5-2004
19.	Dr Y.S. Rajasekhara Reddy	13-5-2004 – 2-9-2009
20.	K Rosaiah	3-9-2009 – 24-11-2010
21.	N Kiran Kumar Reddy	25-11-2010 –

DINNER IN A PANTRY

In 1959, I was appointed director of the department of information of Andhra Pradesh. One of the officers in the department was a dapper young man called Maharaj Karan. He belonged to a premier noble family of Hyderabad. His ancestor, Sagar Mall had come with the first Nizam to Hyderabad in 1724. Sagar Mall was the custodian of the revenue records of the state. So the family came to be known as 'Malwala'. It had a vast estate. It was also given the permission to use the prefix of Raja or Rai and the suffix of Asaf Jahi to their name. The mansion of the family, constructed in 1845 was called Malwala Palace. A durbar for the Kayasths was held there on Dassehra when the traditional tools of the Kayasths - pen and inkpot - were worshipped. The family gave out alms on Muslim festivals and the mansion was illuminated on the birthday of Prophet Muhammad.[83]

The late B. Ramakrishna Rao was a *vakil* of the Malwala estate. On becoming the first popular chief minister of Hyderabad, he took Maharaj Karan as his private secretary.

The Buddha Statue at Hussain Sagar Lake, Hyderabad

Once my wife and I were invited to the Malwala Palace for dinner. We arrived punctually at eight – the time given on the card. There was no sign of the host or hostess there. We saw a servant and asked him whether there was a dinner there. He replied casually in the local lingo, 'Hau Saab'.

'Where is the saab?' I then enquired.

'He is taking water bath,' he replied.

By then we had learnt that the Hyderabadis took bath with water. We still do not know whether they have an alternative way of doing so.

'Please come with me, sir,' he said and led us up a wooden staircase to the first floor. From there we passed through a long wooden gallery the walls of which were decorated with coat-of-arms, trophies, swords, matchlocks, and helmets from old time finally reaching a hall. Two large chandeliers threw gentle light on the stained glass windows and carved furniture. The furniture was old style and portraits of generations of patriarchs looked down upon us stiffly.

Interior of Malwala Palace

After about half-an-hour, Maharaj Karan appeared on the scene. Almost half bent and wringing his hands as if drying them after his wet bath, he apologised for the delay and calmed us down with stories of his ancestors.

About nine o'clock, the first pair of guests strolled in. Then an irregular stream of guests started arriving. A liveried bearer went around with a tray full of a variety of drinks. Being a teetotaller, I took a soft drink. One disadvantage of soft drinks is that you cannot have too many of them. Therefore, while other guests were becoming jollier by the minute, I kept sipping the juice as slowly as possible and was becoming duller. Because of that, I felt generally neglected.

Guests continued to amble in till well past ten. Both my wife and I had started feeling hungry by then. I gathered courage to ask the host when the dinner would be served. Maharaj Karan looked at me with great surprise. 'It is only *ten*, Sir' he said, 'dinner will be served in due course.' I waited for another hour, and then, in sheer exasperation said, 'Look we are famished and can't wait any longer.'

Maharaj Karan suggested coolly that if we wanted to have dinner so early, he could have us fed in the pantry. After that, we could slip away unnoticed.

So my wife and I ate in the pantry amidst cooks, other servants, and piles of utensils and crockery being washed and dried for the dinner. The cooks and bearers brushed past us wondering whether we were food samplers.

That incident was instructive. Thenceforth we decided that in Hyderabad we should never go to a dinner before ten. Now, generally, we go to dinners after having a proper meal at home but leaving enough appetite for pudding. It was at that party that I tasted *nimish* for the first time. This sweet is made of the fluff of boiled milk kept in earthen cups overnight in the open. It was so delicious that I took many helpings hoping that it was not noticed.

The Malwala family had a special license to distil liquor. They made exotic drinks of all types. One particular wine, made of anise seed, claimed to be a sure remedy for asthma. I must confess that I did taste that specialty. Generously, I exempted such experimental drinking from teetotalism.

Maharaj Karan was a personification of social graces. He was never out of his depth in any company and so the government always deputed him to receive and attend upon foreign VIPs. He would even take them home and entertain them. In his hospitality, he went 'beyond the call of duty'.

I stayed in that department for five years. In the beginning, Maharaj would give a ten or five rupee note to his attender to get a packet of cigarettes and did not take the remaining amount. All the attenders therefore wanted to catch his eye for such errands. As time passed, he started taking back the paper currency leaving the loose change as a tip. Then a time came when he would take the whole change back as a matter of course. Just like any one of us.

That transition reflected the declining fortunes of the landed gentry.

After his father's death, the main part of the mansion and the central court were converted into a 'function hall'. The decrepit state of the building was marred further by garish paints and dazzling multi-coloured lights. Its depressing ambience was enhanced by the loud band and filmy music. We attended a wedding there and passed through bare creaking galleries which once flaunted arms and trophies on their walls. Malwala Palace underlined more than anything, the passage of the unkind years for the old nobility.

Our last visit was in August 1996 when the morning papers brought us the sad news of Maharaj Karan's passing away. A large number of relatives and friends had gathered to pay their last respects to the man whose body lay in the dewan khana exactly below a missing chandelier.

As the mourners dispersed, I realised that we would never visit the Malwala Palace again. For us, one of the old monuments with personal associations had disappeared from the map of the city. Sometime later, it was sold away. Then the anonymous buyer demolished it and built a multi-storied complex in its place.

Time devours all.

WHAT IS THERE IN A NAME?

T. Anjaiah was probably the only chief minister of Andhra Pradesh (1980-1982) who rose from the very bottom to the very top. He started his career as a daily-wage labourer in the now defunct Allwyn Steel Factory. He never tried to hide his humble origin. On the other hand, he used to mention it proudly in many public meetings so that the audience should not expect much sophistication from him. Naturally, he did not appreciate music and other fine arts very much. This incident occurred at a Spic-Macay concert in an open ground. The ground was overfull because the renowned duo of classical music, the late Pandit Ravi Shankar, and Ustad Allah Rakha were to do a *jugal bandi* on sitar and tabla.

T Anjaiah

Anjaiah was the chief guest for the occasion. He came very late much after the concert had already started. After his arrival, as is customary, he was requested by the organisers to 'say a few words.'

Anjaiah apologised for his late arrival and confessed to his lack of knowledge of the subject.

However, he extended a warm welcome to the renowned maestros. While referring to them he mixed up the name of Allah Rakha and called him 'Allah-Ho-Akbar.' The audience broke into loud laughter at this faux pas.

Anjaiah looked perplexed and asked, 'Have I said anything wrong?' One of his aides whispered into his ear, that he had not taken the correct name of the tabla maestro. Thereupon Anjaiah said casually, 'Oh, does it matter? After all Allah Rakha and Allah-ho-Akbar are not very different.'

That raised more peals of laughter.

HERO AS CHIEF MINISTER

N.T. Rama Rao was a top actor in Telugu films. He had played the role of most Hindu mythological heroes beside lead roles in many social films with a variety of themes. He was a household name and many people in the state used to worship his image as a god in their homes. He captured the political stage on the wave of his enormous popularity. He became chief minister of Andhra Pradesh for the first time in 1983. However, his handicap was his absolute lack of understanding of the complexities of political and social issues. It was therefore a big job for bureaucracy to adjust to his style of working. The first problem was his working hours. His official day started at 5.30 a.m. He summoned senior officers from that time onwards. Appointments were given and meetings were fixed very early in the day.

For laying foundation stones, which he had to do often, he would specify the type of stone and where it could be obtained from. His ego was naturally enormous and his eccentricities unending. Once he started wearing a ring in one ear, then he started saffron clothes and turban in the style of Vivekananda.

Even in official meetings if someone mentioned the implications and risks involved in some of his policy ideas, NTR as he was popularly called, would stand up and remind the small gathering that he was the representative of six-and-a-half crores of Andhras! Ministers rarely opened their mouth before him although they were fully briefed. Secretaries had to do whatever talking was required.

When I was first introduced to him on his assumption of authority, he said. 'Oh, yes. I know him very well.' That was not a good note to start on because I had fiercely opposed his proposal to establish a studio by the side of the Hussain Sagar Lake.

He was used to solving problems on the screen within three hours, and in mythological films by a mere swish of a hand. He expected as in his historical films, ministers and civil servants only to say, 'Yes, Sir.'

In his election speeches, he had been saying that he would reduce the plethora of corporations and boards. The chief secretary told him that I had proposed abolitions and merger of about sixty odd bodies. 'Very good,' he said, 'Tell me.'

I picked up the file and said, 'Sir, I think that the number of corporations could be reduced from about sixty to twenty-three.'

'No,' he said, 'it should be thirteen.'

I said, 'I have worked out and have arrived at this number…'

'Show me,' he interrupted me. I gave him a copy of the list I had prepared.

We started with housing. He went over the list of proposed abolitions and mergers from nine to three. Suddenly he said, 'Warehousing Corporation should also be merged with the Housing Corporation.'

I submitted that it had nothing in common with Housing Corporation.

He said, 'No, *housing* is common!'

I could not argue further.

During his visit to America for his bypass surgery, he had seen Disneyland. On return, he wanted to set up a similar amusement park. At that time, the import of equipment for amusement parks was banned. I was handling Tourism. I explained that point to him. He said, 'We will get the policy relaxed. You go and meet the prime minister.' I said I was too small a fry to even ask for an appointment. He said, 'You go and tell him that you represent the chief minister of Andhra Pradesh.' I took it as a joke and came out of the meeting.

A week later, I happened to be present in another meeting. Suddenly, he asked me, 'Have you been to Delhi?' I asked what for, Sir. He said I told you to go and meet the prime minister. His secretary winked at me and told him that he would look into that. Ultimately, my minister, a lady, NTR's political adviser, the late Upendra, and I went to Delhi and met the minister of state for Finance. When Upendra raised the point he said, 'Now what does Mr Drama Rao want?' After that, we all talked about the weather over coffee and we came out.

N.T. Rama Rao

One early morning while I was still asleep my phone rang. I looked at the watch. It was 5 a.m. I picked up the receiver and uttered a somewhat annoyed hello. The voice said, 'This is Rama Rao speaking.'

Rama Rao was the name of one of my colleagues. I said. 'Rama Rao, what's happened? Why this call so early in the morning?'

The voice became authoritative, 'This is the *chief minister* speaking.'

Normally, some PA rings up and tells you that the chief minister is coming on the line. You have some time to gather your thoughts.

'Sorry, Sir, I did not recognise your voice on the phone.'

'No problem,' he said, 'I just wanted to tell you that I like your ideas on tourism. Very good.'

'Thank you, Sir,' I said wondering at the reason for the unexpected compliment. And he put down the receiver.

He was egotistic and eccentric. He could also be gracious - and suddenly turn around the other way. Which did happen one day.

THE CHARMING LINGO OF HYDERABADIS

The *potta* and *potti* language of the Deccan may be the cause of amusement elsewhere in the country. But in Hyderabad it is not only a staple of everyday conversation, it is also a matter of semantics. There is a world of difference between *haula* and *hallu*, *nakko* and *hau*!

If there is any one factor across the country, which rouses laughter about the Hyderabadi, it is the peculiar language spoken by him. We now call it a dialect but once it was an accepted language formed by the fusion of the Aryan language, Marathi, with the Dravidian languages, Kannada and Telugu. Prof Maud Hussain Khan calls it proto-Urdu, that is, old Urdu. All the early poets of the Deccan including Mohammed Quli Qutb Shah, the founder of Hyderabad, Mulla Wajahi, Nusrati, Gawwasi and other prose writers used this language.

The original base of Dakhni is Punjabi. Briefly, the clash - or fusion - of Persian and Punjabi which occurred with the invasion and prolonged occupation of the Punjab by the Persian-speaking sultans, Mahmud Ghaznavi and Muhammad Ghori, from 1020 CE onwards gave birth to a language which later came to be called Urdu. It was 173 years before a sultan sat on the throne of Delhi in 1193. Another century was to elapse before the sultan of Delhi, Allaudin Khilji, attacked the south, and conquered the Kakatiya and other kingdoms. It was Urdu, which came down with that army to the Deccan. In 1347, the local chieftains appointed by the Delhi sultan revolted against Muhammad Tughlaq and set up the Bahmani kingdom. Their language, called Dakhni, got trapped here, because the Bahmanis did not want to have anything to do with the north. The next development took place in 1687 when Aurangzeb conquered Golkonda and the Urdu of the north came to influence Dakhni.

To the unaccustomed ear, Dakhni sounds quaint. For many years I wondered why it sounded so familiar in parts and why some of the words were the same which my grandmothers used but which were not familiar to our generation. Then one day I found the antecedents of Dakhni and its link with my own mother-tongue. Of the 2466 words in the glossary of Dakhni terms appended by Dr Syeda Jaffar to her anthology of Mohd. Quli Qutb Shah, 41 per cent were Punjabi![84]

Today Dakhni poets elicit laughter by merely reciting their poems in Urdu *mushairas* even when the subject is serious. Sarvar Danda with his satirical poem 'Sanjiva Reddy Mama' was hilarious and Suleman Khatib with his poems on the plight of lower middle class women moved audiences to tears. Himayatullah does both in a few poems he is asked to recite repeatedly. Pagal Adilabadi, Talib Khumdmiri and Mustafa Ali Baig cause convulsions of laughter in the audience, especially Baig with his Anglo-Urdu poems.

The influence of Telugu on Dakhni can be seen in words like '*kate*' which is '*kahte*' in Urdu and '*anta*', the ending generally given to statements in Telugu. It is like saying 'they say' or 'it is said'. That way the responsibility for a statement is diffused, and one can never be pinned down. The Marathi suffix '*ch*' is used for adding emphasis – like *'wohi ch'* – 'just that'. When they want to say yes, they say *'hau'* instead of the *'han'* of normal Urdu.

'Hallu' is 'slowly' or 'carefully'. *'Haula'* on the other hand is for 'daft'. The question 'why' in its infinite variations is conveyed in Dakhni by *'kaiko'*. 'Don't' and variations of the negative imperative are all contained in the expression *'nakko'* (of Marathi origin). The plural is constructed in the same way as in Punjabi and sometimes as in Persian, but not as in Urdu.

Charming Telengana women in a rage curse with utmost ferocity, in Dakhni. *'Matti pade'* means 'may earth fall upon you' or 'may you be under the earth' – capital punishment in effect. The young and 'inferiors' are supposed to greet elders and superiors by bending so low that their heads touch the latters' belly. The interesting expression for this posture is *'pet mein mundi dalna'* – *mundi* being head. That makes it easy for the elder to bless the youngster by placing his hand on his head or both shoulders.

Apart from these grammatical and linguistic peculiarities, the Hyderabadi's sense of time is geological. An interval of two days for a Hyderabadi can embrace a century – or even longer. Consequently, they use *'parson'* (the day before yesterday) for anything, which happened generations ago. When I was new to Hyderabad, many people often referred to the *'parsoon ki tughyani* – the deluge of the day before yesterday. I scanned all the papers, and checked with many people and found that in no part of the city or even the state had there been any floods lately! Then it was explained to me, rather matter-of-factly, that the reference obviously was to the great deluge of 1908, which had destroyed one-third of the city. Anything, which had ever happened in the past, happened only the day before yesterday for Hyderabadis. Which must be a convenient way of disposing of a lot of junk called history.

It is perhaps the same attitude to time which makes a man of fifty refer to another of the same age in absentia as a '*potta*' (Telugu for boy) and '*potti*' for girl or just '*baccha*' for a child or a young man.

Another interesting feature, which is now on the wane, is that many women, particularly from the upper classes, refer to themselves in the masculine gender. I was quite foxed in the beginning when a perfectly normal looking female referred to herself as male. I asked my wife to check her identity and she reported that indeed my interlocutor had all the visible attributes of women. Nobody as yet has been able to give me a satisfactory explanation for this mixing of the genders. Perhaps they took it from one of the world's first women's brigades, described earlier in Bedtime Stories – The Amazons of the Nizams.

The northerner is so fascinated by the way Dakhni is spoken that my children

used to be teased by our relatives on our holidays in the north just to get a spontaneous response from them in Dakhni. When my son was asked to do something unreasonable, he would be cut to the quick and ask '*kaiko*?' and everybody would laugh on hearing that. That led him to say '*nakko*' to them, which led to further guffaws. No wonder that my children believe till today that northerners are not half as cultured as Hyderabadis.

Dakhni is still spoken, but increasingly it is being confined to the lower classes. Even the elite often slip into Dakhni, though they are reluctant to admit it. The following story is often narrated to underline the linguistic paradox of the upper classes.

Once a stranger to the city asked whether the road he was standing on led to Charminar. An urchin replied '*hau*.' A respectable middle class Hyderabadi passerby overheard this. He called the boy and admonished him for using the vulgar expression '*hau*.'

'Yes, Sir,' the boy noted respectfully and asked, 'what should I have said?'

'*Ji Han*,' replied the senior citizen gravely.

'So *hau* is a vulgar word?' the boy asked by way of confirmation.

'*Hau*,' replied the elder involuntarily!

Hyderabad is divided into zones of various languages though Dakhni has blurred these linguistic boundaries, giving the state its composite culture. Though reduced to a dialect, it still rules supreme, and is responsible for much of the charm of the old city.

It is not as if Dakhni is not serious. Note the concentrated wisdom in the following proverbs:

The charming lingo of Hyderabadis *(courtesy Subhani)*

Phoophi sas nakko
Bhatiji bahu nakko
Bandi sautan nakko
Khet mein nala nakko
Ghar mein sala nakko
Kathil pital ka saz nakko
Boodhe mard ka raj nakko

(Father's sister should not be mother-in-law
Brother's daughter should not be daughter-in-law
Maid should not be made a co-wife
Sown land should not have a drain
Wife's brother should not stay in the house
Brass ornaments are useless, Just as marriage with an old man is pointless.)[85]

THE WAY WE ARE

While clouds were gathering on the horizon and life was becoming difficult in the districts, the city of Hyderabad retained its surface poise, charm, and attraction.

Philip Mason of the Indian Civil Service, who visited Hyderabad in March 1947 and stayed here for a few weeks before leaving India could not resist describing the cosmopolitan character and even tenor of the life of the city.

> 'It was someone's birthday and the children were playing *Oranges and Lemons*. Uncle Yusuf and Aunt Fatima held up their hands to make an arch; they were enjoying themselves as much as the children and Uncle Yusuf seemed to have forgotten that he was a member of the Cabinet and that he was formally addressed by a tremendous title that meant he was a leader in battle and victorious in war. "Here comes a chopper to CHOP off his head!" Their hands came down and they had caught a merry struggling little urchin who was trying to escape. *Oranges or Lemons*? they whispered in his ear and with peals of laughter, he joined the tug-of-war team behind Aunt Fatima.

> 'Who is that little boy?' I asked my nearest neighbour and she told me a name I have forgotten, but a name unmistakably Hindu, some Ram Swarup or Jag Deo.
>
> 'But he's wearing the wrong sort of hat!' I exclaimed in astonishment. He was wearing a Turkish fez, like an inverted red plant pot with a black silk tassel, which in Northern India was always the sign of a Muslim. 'Oh, here in Hyderabad we do not care for things like that!' said my neighbour gaily. 'It is one of the nice things here that we are so delightfully cosmopolitan.'[86]

After the Police Action, all officials of the State – especially the Muslims – were subjected to a quick screening. Some were removed, some reduced in rank, while others were allowed to continue. Some were even put in jail pending investigation.

Late in October 1948, a festival day, General Choudhuri summoned all secretaries and heads of departments of the Hyderabad government for a conference at the Bolarum Residency. He wanted to chat with some of them individually and make his own assessment with the help of the dossiers which had been prepared on various officers and given to him. Amongst them was Rai Janaki Pershad who was at the time the acting director of the information and public relations department. He was surprised to see many of the officers who had always sported beards and wore *sherwanis*, clean-shaven and in western suits. Pershad went in his usual *sherwani* and *Roomi* cap. Officials were called by the ADC to the military governor, Captain Pyare Lal, one by one. He would peep into the waiting room and call the name politely, as nurses do in clinics. 'Mr Rai

Janaki Pershad,' the ADC called softly, not knowing that the prefix of Mr was superfluous with Rai. As the officer got up and made for the door, the ADC stopped him. 'Not you, yet.' He sat down. Nobody else got up. He then looked at the list and called the next name. Habeebur Rehman went in. The ADC came out again as Rehman emerged from his interview, and called, 'Mr Rai Janaki Pershad.' Janaki Pershad got up and began to make for the door with all the dignity at his command. The ADC was a little annoyed at this impatient, intrusive official. 'Not you, Sir.' he said brusquely. 'I want Mr Rai Janaki Pershad.'

'I am Rai Janaki Pershad,' replied the officer in a somewhat offended tone.

'Oh!' Captain Pyare Lal exclaimed, 'Then why are you dressed like a Muslim?'

'This is the way we dress here,' replied Janaki Pershad coolly.

The ADC smiled in embarrassment and ushered the officer in. He was being acquainted with the spirit of Hyderabad, which stood him in good stead for the rest of his stay in the city.[87]

A decade later when I landed in Hyderabad, we became friends with many people including a young

Rai Janaki Pershad

charming Hyderabadi lady, Lakshmi Devi Raj. She wore a dot on her head but whenever she left, she would bid good-bye in the old Hyderabadi style: '*Khuda Hafiz*'.

One day my mother, who hailed from Lahore and had come to India as a refugee after the Partition, saw her doing that. After her departure, she asked me, 'This woman – is she a Hindu or a Muslim?'

'Why? Of course, she is Hindu. Don't you know her name?'

'But then why does she say '*Khuda Hafiz*?' she asked, her confusion persisting.

'Everyone says that here,' I told her.

Next time, when Lakshmi bade my mother good-bye, my mother too responded with '*Khuda Hafiz.*'

EPILOGUE

And so on and on we can go. There are other aspects to the city's persona. Quaint eponymy, and cuisine which is so varied that pickles and chutneys alone number thirty-three, while desserts go up to seventy-six![88] A sense of humour so refined that they make themselves their own but....The list is endless.

I have been here for over half a century and yet my surprises are not over. Sarojini Naidu, the most illustrious daughter of the city rightly proclaimed that Hyderabad invests its people with a subtle kinship whose claims have been seldom denied.

If you found the stories narrated in this book credible, consider the results of my private survey.

Out of every ten persons who visit Hyderabad, twelve come back and settle down in Hyderabad.

What? Bad arithmetic? No, it is ten of those original group and two more whom they convince to come along.

That is the fatal charm of Hyderabad!

Notes & References

1. National Geophysical Research Institute; Department of Mining and Geology, A.P.; Narendra Luther, *Rockscape of Andhra Pradesh (2012).*
2. *Travels of the Abbe Carre in India and the Near East, 1672-74.* tr. from Ms. by Lady Fawcett. (1947).
3. Ferishta, *History of the Rise of Mohammedan Power in India.* Vol. III. tr. John Gibbs. (1829).
4. Jean de Thevenot *Travels into the Levant.* Vol. III tr. A. Lovel. (1687).
5. H.G. Briggs, The Nizam–*His History and Relations with the British Government.* Vol. II. (1861)
6. S.H. Bilgrami and C. Wilmot. *History and Descriptive Sketches of H.H. the Nizam's Dominions.* Vol. II. 1883.
7. Jan Pieper, 'A Quranic Interpretation in Architectural Metaphor' in 'Environmental Design': *The Journal of the Islamic Design Research Centre.* Special Issue. January (1983).
8. Hakim Nizamuddin Geelani, *Hadiqatus Salateen.* 1053 H. tr. Ghulam Ahmed Sarvar (1986).
9. Server-ul-Mulk, *Karnama-e-Sarvari.* tr. Jeevan Yar Jung. (u.d.)
10. H.K. Sherwani, *History of Medieval Deccan 1295-1724* (1974).
11. Shah Rocco, *Golkonda and the Qutb Shahs* (1929)
12. Khafi Khan, *Muntakhib-ul-Lubab.* (1874).
13. K.V. Bhoopala Rao, *The Illustrious Prime Minster Madanna* (1984).
14. Mohd. Suleman Siddiqui, 'Two neglected Chishti saints of Golkonda' in M .L. Nigamed. *Glimpses of Qutb Shahi Culture* (1986).
15. S.M.Q. Zore, *Sair-e-Golkonda* (1940).
16. Bhoopala Rao, *The Illustrious Prime Minister Madanna.* (1984).
17. Quoted by Rahat Azmi in 'Noor Khan Ka Bazaar' in *Hyderabad ke Mohalle.* Siasat Publications No. 19. (1990).
18. Mansa Ram, *Ma'asir-Nizami* Persian Ms. Quoted by P. Sethu Madhava Rao. *Eighteenth Century Deccan.* (1963).

19. Ibid.
20. John William Kaye, *Life and Correspondence of Major General John Malcolm.* (1856).
21. H. G. Brigg, *The Nizam–His History and Relations with the British Government.* (1861).
22. Mohd. Sirajuddin Talib, *Mir Alam ki Swaneh Zindagi* (1930)
23. Ghulam Samdani Bidri, *Gulzar-e- Mah Laqa.* (1834); Shafqat Razvi, *Mah Laqa Bai Chanda.* (1950); S.H. Bilgrami and C. Wilmot.
24. Kenneth Ballhatchet, *Race Sex and Class under the Raj–Imperial Attitudes and their Critics. 1793-1905.* (1985).
25. Narendra Luther, *Lashkar–The Story of Secunderabad.* (2010).
26. A photocopy of these documents is available with the author.
27. SMQ Zore, *Kulliyat-e-Mohd. Quli Qutb Shah.* (1940); Couplet tr. Narendra Luther.
28. Sever-ul-Mulk.
29. Ibid.
30. Moulvi Sayyad Amjid Ali Ashahari, *Swaneh Umri Ala Hazrat Mehboob Ali Khan.* (1911).
31. Note by Dr A. Ramachari, one-time director of department of history of medicine, Hyderabad; R.J. Rajendra Prasad, 'Chloroform Controversy-A Century Ago', *The Hindu*, 1 May 1988.
32. E.F. Dodd, *Sir Ronald Ross and his Fight Against Malaria.* (1956); R.L. Megroz, *Ronald Ross Discoverer and Creator* (1931); Paper from the Department of History of Medicine, Hyderabad.
33. Archduke Ferdinand Franz. *My Journey around the World* tr. Elizabeth Al-Himrani. (1996).
34. Sibte Hasan, *Shehar-e- Nigaaraan.* (1984).
35. Mujtaba Hussain, *Hyderabad Ke Kisse Kahaniyan aur Rawaayaat.* (1994).
36. Sidq Jaisi, *Durbaar-e-Dürbaar.* (1994); tr. Luther. *The Nocturnal Court.* (2004).
37. Narendra Luther, *Raja Deen Dayal–Prince of Photography.* (2006).
38. For a history of Samasthans, see Benjamin B. Cohen, *Kingship and Colonialism in India's Deccan 1850-1948.* (2007)
39. Family source. (1995).
40. Mehdi Nawaz Jung. *Maharaja Kishen Pershad.* 1950; Habeeb Zia, *Maharaja Sir Kishen Pershad Shad Hayaat aur Adabi Kaarname* (1978); Mehdi Nawaz Jung, *Maharaja Kishen Pershad* (1950); Dr. Narayan Raj and Prof. Habeeb Zia eds., *Nazar-e-Shad* (2009).
41. Raman Raj Saxena, Tazkara-e–Durbar–e-Hyderabad. (1998).
42. Mansa Ram.
43. Nawab Mehdi Nawaz Jung.
44. Raja Rameshwar Rao to the author 1990.

45. Sibte-e-Hasan; Interview with Al Ahmed Jaleeli July 1994.
46. Sibte Hasan; Luther, 'Poet and Publisher'. *The Hindu* 19 September 1998.
47. H.E.H. the Nizam's Trust. (2013)
48. A copy of the speech and of the news reported in *The Hindu* was made available to the author by his son, the late Prof. Rasheedudin Khan along with a covering letter.
49. As narrated to the author by Jeelani Pairak on 14 November 1994.
50. Mirza Zafarul Hasan, *Zikr-e-Yar Chale* (1979); Mahirul Qadri, 'Yad-e-Raftgan' in 'Faran Monthly, April 1967.
51. Sidq Jaisi.
52. Ms. Note given to the author by his grandson on 19 August 1992; K. P. S. Menon, *Many Worlds Revisited–An Autobiography* (1981); Luther, 'Wit-laureate of Hyderabad', *The Hindu*, 15 January 1998.
53. Mirza Zafar-ul-Hasan, *Zikr-e-Yar Chale* (1979).
54. Nazeer-ud-Din Ahmed, *Swaneh Bahadur Yar Jung* (1998).
55. Notes and picture provided by Ismet Mehdi, daughter-in-law of Nawab Mehdi Nawaz Jung.
56. Maulana Abul Kalam Azad Oriental Research Institute Hyderabad, *Nawab Mehdi Nawaz Jung Memorial Volume.* (1972).
57. There are a number of books, articles, and documents on this subject. Principally, one should look up *Tareekh-e-Majlis–e-Ittehad–ul–Musalmeen* (1941); Mir Laik Ali, *Tragedy of Hyderabad;* Freed Mirza, *Pre- and Post Police Action Days in the Erstwhile Hyderabad State–What I saw. felt and did* (1976); Zafarul Hasan, *Deccan Udas Hai Yaro,* Vol. III (1976); K. M. Munshi *The End of an Era – (Hyderabad Memoirs)* (1957); Omar Khalidi ed. *Hyderabad after the Fall* (1998); Lucien D Benichou, *From Autocracy to Integration–Political Developments in Hyderabad State (1938-1948)* (2000); V.K. Bawa, *The Last Nizam* (1991); Mohammad Hyder, *October Coup–A Memoir of the Struggle for Hyderabad* (2012) etc. I also interviewed several persons, most important of whom was Zahid Ali Kamil, advocate and the most faithful and steadfast follower of Kasim Razvi. He was then 81. I had several sittings with him starting on 25 August 1992.
58. Mohammad Abdul Hai, ed. *Mamlakat-e- Asafiya,* Vol. 1, published by the first generation of emigrants from Hyderabad to Pakistan, Idara-e-Mohibban-e-Deccan (1978).
59. Narrated by the last Controller Radio Deccan circa 1962.
60. K.M. Munshi.
61. Mohd. Murtuza Ali Khan, ed. *Suraagh Rasaani aur Taftish* (u.d); The Hyderabad Law Reports 1951, *Case of Showkat- un -Nissa & Nine others Vs. The State of Hyderabad 1950.*

62. Interview with B.P.R. Vithal 5 August 1992.
63. Based on a note and picture given by Ismet Mehdi; Luther: 'Jai Hind Safrani' in The Hindu 20 October 2000. The story was included in the text book for Class VII of Delhi Schools by the State Educational and Research Council.
64. Interview with Mehdi Ali 2 July 1992.
65. *Felicitation Volume for Ravi Narayan Reddy (*1983); Interview with his daughter, Prof. Ravi Bharati Reddy 18 August 1992, and with Chandra Rajeshwar Rao, former General Secretary of the Communist Party of India 26 August 1992.
66. Residency Records of Hyderabad in the National Archives of India. File No. F 392 - P/47 of 1947; Michael H. Fisher, *Indirect Rule in India* (1991); Harriet Ronken Lynton, *My dear Nawab Saheb* (1991);
67. Hashim Amir Ali, 'The Last of Salar Jungs: Personal Reminiscences of a Bygone Era'. S. J. M. Biannual Journal Vol. IX - X - 1976-77
68. Interview with Rao. (65 supra).
69. 'Kishen Documents' in *History of the Communist Party* Vol. VII; P. Sunadrayya, *Telangana People's Struggle and its Lessons.* tr. Desraj Chadda (1972); Mallikarjuna Sharma, ed. *In Retrospect* Vol. 5 (2002); Mohit Sen, *A Traveller and the Road –The Journey of an Indian Communist.* (2003). Interviews with Rao (67 supra) and Raj Bahadur Gour 11 August 1992.
70. J.D.B. Gribble.
71. Philip Meadows Taylor, *The Story of My Life.* (1920).
72. Server–ul-Mulk.
73. K.V. Ranga Reddy, *The Struggle and the Betrayal.* tr. K. Ramchandra Reddy (2010).
74. Luther, *Lashkar- The Story of Secunderabad.* (2010)
75. Ascribed to Shibli Yazdani by Mohd. Nuruddin Khan in 'Sabras' Urdu monthly issue of June 1995.
76. Sibte Hasan.
77. Interview with Col. Khusro Yar Khan 24 January 1994. He fought on the eastern front during the Police Action in 1948.
78. Interview with S. N. Bilgrami 12 September 1992.
79. Usha Raman, ed. *Disha Guides-Hyderabad.* (1991).
80. Sir Mirza Ismail, *My Public Life: Recollections and Reflections.* (1954); Hosh Bilgrami, *Mushahdat* (1950).
81. Interviews with Syed Hashim Ali 12 September 1992 and subsequent days
82. Interview with Ali Pasha, son-in-law of Nizam VII, 8 April 1994.

83. Karen Isaksen Leonard, *Social History of an Indian Caste–The Kayasths of Hyderabad* (1994); Sheela Raj, *Portrait of an Era–Hyderabad in the days of the Nizams 1828-1896.* (1996); Narendra Luther. 'Dinner in a Pantry', Economic Times, Hyderabad 31 August 1997.
84. Syeda Jaffar, *Kulliyat- e- Mohammad Quli Qutb Shah* (1985); Narendra Luther, 'Confusing Fusion' in *Power of Glory* (1998).
85. I am indebted to Dr. Oudesh Rani Bawa for introducing me to these and similar proverbs.
86. Philip Mason, *A Shaft of Sunlight: Memoirs of a Varied Life* (1978).
87. Interview with Mohan Prasad 10 July 1992. He is Rai Janaki Pershad's son who drove his father to the meeting.
88. Mohammad Abdul Hai.

INDEX